PRAISE FOR
I WASN'T READY TO SAY GOODBYE

"As one who deals with unexpected death, I am so pleased to find a truly valuable reference for those souls who are blindsided by such misery. I would characterize this work as thoughtful, thorough, and intensely meaningful. The personal passages, which share feelings and experiences . . . are superb. They turn a scholarly treatise into one that will touch those in suffering greatly and help them understand the wide range of emotions that they will experience. Up until now, Rabbi Kushner's reference, *When Bad Things Happen to Good People*, has been my mainstay in such circumstances; I will add this book to my recommended list to loved ones and friends."

>*E. Charles Douville, MD,*
>*Cardiothoracic Surgeon,*
>*Providence Portland Hospital*

"Noel and Blair's *I Wasn't Ready to Say Goodbye* ranks right up there with *When Bad Things Happen to Good People* to help people deal with the sudden loss of a loved one. Particularly helpful is the degree of permissiveness to grieve in one's own unique way without regarding it as pathological in a supportive and nonjudgmental way. It is informative and practical, yet personal and warm. It is both practical and instructive, taking a developmental approach to grieve with the understanding that one doesn't simply "get over it," but deals at various stages down the road. I particularly like the sections devoted to children and to special occasions and challenges as these are frequently overlooked in these kinds of books. I highly recommend it."

>*Edward S. Beck, EdD,*
>*Harrisburg, PA,*
>*Mental Help.Net*

"*I Wasn't Ready to Say Goodbye* is a book that is easily related to by anyone struggling to cope with the sudden death of a loved one. I highly recommend this book, not only to the bereaved, but to friends and counselors as well. If you want to experience what the pain of grief is like, to better understand what the bereaved are going through, read this book."

>*Helen fitzgerald, author of* **The Grieving Child,**
>**The Mourning Handbook,** *and* **The Grieving Teen**

"This book does an excellent job of addressing a topic that most people choose not to address until they are directly confronted. Grief has a tendency to creep up in the odd hours of the day and the night and can be overwhelming to those experiencing loss. To have a title, a book that you can reach out and grab at any hour offers comfort. I wish this title had been available sooner as it often was a book that comforted and calmed me most during my own deep dark hours of despair. Written from knowledge and from a place of understanding and guidance is sure to make this book a winner and a timeless treasure for anyone who has known a deep loss. This book is excellent and necessary."

Bernadette Moyers,
author of **Angel Stacey**

"The authors have captured a means of discussing and exploring a very painful life passage in real life, down to earth language, and experience. Many thanks to Pam and Brook for having strength to get through their sudden loss of a loved one, wisdom to understanding the Way, and the generosity in sharing their discoveries to further our healing."

Charlotte A. Tomaino, PhD,
Neuropsychologist

"Finally, you have found a friend who can not only explain what has just occurred, but can take you by the hand and lead you to a place of healing and personal growth. Whether you are dealing with the loss of a family member, a close personal associate or a friend, this guide can help you survive and cope, but even more importantly . . . heal."

The Rebecca Review

"This book, by women who have done their homework on grief, offers a companion for others still recuperating. Further, it introduces us to so many others, both famous and ordinary, who can hold a hand and comfort a soul through grief's wilderness. Outstanding references of where to seek other help."

George C. Kandle,
Pastoral Psychotherapist

"A well written book about a very difficult subject. *I Wasn't Ready to Say Goodbye* will be useful for those going through these difficult times."

Bradley Evans, MD,
Cardiologist, Providence Portland Hospital

"As an emergency department nurse with fifteen-plus years experience in that area, I have had first hand experience with sudden death. I have always felt that not enough has been written to address the problems and difficulties that face those who have experienced sudden death/loss, and how it differs from a loss that can be anticipated. This book carefully pointed out the many ways we may grieve, but also gently addressed that point at which the grieving process was no longer healthy and that professional counseling was needed. The overall feeling from this book was of gentleness, guidance, and a sense of spirituality. The reader is given choices, resources, and suggestions to enable them to plan and implement their own grief process. I am planning an in-service education program for the emergency dept. staff (MDs and RNs) on sudden death and grief reduction and will share your book. The list of resources is very comprehensive and it is evident that much time and energy was spent to provide the reader with a very complete guide."

Kathleen Reilly; RN MS CEN

"*I Wasn't Ready to Say Goodbye* is the best non-religious book I have read on grieving from an unexpected death. The authors have direct experience with the subject and share their own deep traumas . . . they also sought out stories different from their own so that you would have specific examples that come closer to your own situation. I found the book to be "right on" in describing the issues that my family and I have dealt with."

Donald Mitchell,
Amazon Top 10 Reviewer

"*I Wasn't Ready to Say Goodbye* by Noel & Blair is just beautiful! It is easy to read, yet covers everything a grieving person could possibly be thinking of or be going through. It is sensitive, yet realistic. (Sometimes those two don't go together well, but in this book they do.) The book is empowering and healing, but in baby steps."

Your Life Magazine

"The death of a loved one is always an emotionally difficult experience. When it comes suddenly and unexpectedly it is even more difficult. In *I Wasn't Ready to Say Goodbye* the authors take you through the grieving process as well as learning how to deal with such a tragic loss. For those dealing with the loss of a loved one, or for those who want to help someone who is, this is a highly recommended read."

Midwest Book Review

"What really makes this book a great resource is their hands on approach to dealing with grief. They share research on why we feel the way we do after a loss, but they go on to give us specific actions to take at a time when we NEED someone to guide us to the next step. The authors write in a friendly but knowledgeable style. They don't talk down to us, but also don't talk over our heads with lofty theories and philosophies. I felt as if they were looking me in the eye and saying "THIS is what you can do to help yourself!" During a time of grief this is exactly what we need."

Seeds of Knowledge

"I've seen many books that deal with grief, but none that do it so comprehensively and accessibly! The authors write with that rare combination of personal passion and professional detachment which allows the grieving to find a pathway to health, in their own way, in their own time. I recommend this wonderful resource for those who have lost a loved one through death or divorce, and to the professionals who endeavor to help them."

Mary Kalifon, Cedars-Sinai Los Angeles, and
author of **My Dad Lost His Job**

"There aren't many 'firsts' these days. Most books being published are like so many others. This book, *I Wasn't Ready to Say Goodbye* is a first and it is valuable beyond my ability to describe it. Suffice it to say that it is truly excellent. It understands. It supports. It comforts. It sheds light. It holds your hand. It is there for you, in a time of unbearable anguish and need, like no other book ever written on the subject."

Art Klein,
author of **Dad and Son**

Reader Reviews
"After I lost my son in a tragic accident, this book reinstilled my hope and helped me cope with my heart wrenching grief over a parent's worst nightmare—that of losing a child."

M. Pierce, GA

"I bought this book three years ago when my mom died suddenly. It was such a big help to me to get through the stages of grief. It explained everything that I was feeling and going through at the time. It was a tremendous comfort to me and had a big healing effect. I have since bought it for a few of my friends who have lost their parents, and they have in turn bought it for others."

Iris C.

"This book is currently helping my mom deal with her feelings after the death of my dad a few months back. She picks it up almost every morning before she starts her day. It helps her to understand her feelings and realize that she is 'normal' in her grief. I highly recommend it."

A. Geiger

"This book provided the support and answers I needed at my time of grief. I shared this book with the rest of my family who also found it extremely helpful and easy to read. You will find that you can pick it up and read from any chapter in any order. The explanations are very helpful and the information can be comforting. I would highly recommend this book to anyone grieving the loss of a loved one."

D. Canton, MI

"The examples and special cases of losses by others written and shared in the book help one place themselves in the midst of others' losses and compare and differentiate the circumstances. Sometimes learning about another's more difficult time within your own loss helps get things into perspective. I keep reading and rereading this wonderful book. Each time I review a certain area I find that something else jumps out in regards to "where I am" in my walk with grief that day."

J. Conforti

"*I Wasn't Ready to Say Goodbye* is such a wonderful, wonderful book! To see my thoughts, actions, and feelings of everything that comes along during the grief of a loved one, particularly one lost by a sudden death. I was even comforted by carrying it with me for over a year. Just having it near me helped so that I could read it anytime. I recently loaned it to my best friend who just lost her younger sister to suicide and I actually feel very naked without my copy!

My favorite aunt was murdered by my uncle and then he committed suicide. Trying to deal with it was so hard because I felt there was no one in the world who understood my pain, my fears, my irrational thoughts, "griefbursts," guilt, and that overwhelming feeling of being lost. This book helped me to find my way, to know that everything I was feeling and thinking was completely normal, and just to see it all in print is such a relief. This book teaches you the grief process from just about every point of view possible (parent, child, sibling, friend, etc.), gives you tips on how to cope and memorialize the ones you've lost, advice on where to seek professional help when needed, and the writers tell their own stories of loss and everything they experienced. *I Wasn't Ready to Say Goodbye* mentions the taboos surrounding sudden deaths such as suicide or homicide and lets you know that it's okay to talk about it and that you need to talk about it."

Wyatt, St. Louis, MO

"*I Wasn't Ready to Say Goodbye* offers much practical advice for getting through the immediate days, months, and years following the sudden death of a loved one. For many who experience the unexpected death of a loved one, the shock is so great that the survivors don't even know how to get through the time between the death and the funeral. I know that I fell into this category, and was knocking myself out to try to be "normal" when in fact nothing at all in my family was normal or the same. This book does a great job of explaining practical, small steps to recover from a great loss.

The authors offer the premise that the grief process is a bit different for survivors of a sudden death, when compared to an "expected" death, such as a death from a lingering illness. I did feel that the authors had felt my pain of having a loved one snatched away in a matter of minutes, and talked about the added confusion and anger this sort of death gives the survivors. I found the compassionate tone of the authors and the pragmatic exercises to be extremely helpful."

L. Kelly, CO

"I purchased this book when my step father died suddenly three years ago to help me understand my loss. I now have turned to it again as I'm faced with the sudden death of my seventeen-year-old son to suicide. I highly recommend this book as a starting point for anyone who has lost a loved one or friend suddenly! Thank you Brook and Pamela for your hope."

J. Daniellson, MN

"A friend gave me this book shortly after my younger brother died suddenly at the age of twenty-four. It was a lifesaver—something I could relate to and that could guide me through my grief, even down to details that authors less acquainted with the unique aspects of sudden death grief might not understand. I read it at the beginning and then reread it after several months, when I picked up more helpful advice that I hadn't been ready to notice the first time around. I strongly recommend it to anyone who has the misfortune to find him- or herself coping with the sudden death of a loved one."

Jessica, Princeton, NJ

"I had almost given up in the search for a book which even mentioned sibling grief when I noticed this book in a bookstore. The subtitle in the sibling section "overlooked in the grieving process" caught my eye and for the first time since my sister died more than a year before, I felt less alone. I also found the resource section helpful and have hooked up with a grief support group."

Kit, TX

"I purchased this book at the recommendation of my therapist, along with the companion workbook. She told me that it was like having a "mini support group" that I could access whenever I need it. She was right. Thank you Pam and Brook for caring enough to take your own difficult tragedies and find a way to help others. I have grown so much as a result of working through this book."

Janet, O., TX

"I found this book shortly after my thirty-one-year-old brother, Chad, became the victim of a homicide. What a relief to read that I was not alone in my feelings, that I wasn't going crazy! This book helped me deal with emotions that I had never dealt with before and get through some rough times. I passed it on to my Mother and it is helping her."

Julie L., FL

"This book was a gift and I almost read it from cover to cover the first reading. It covers a lot of important scenarios that I related to. It helped me understand that my bizarre behavior and thoughts were not bizarre after all. It also forewarned me about firsts and gave good suggestions on how to deal with them effectively. Overall, I recommend this book highly."

Judi H., NH

"When I first came across this book, I was hurting so very badly. Mike, my very dearest friend and the man I was in love with had been killed in an accident. I didn't have a chance to say goodbye to him. I hurt so bad that I walked in a blind maze. I really didn't want to live on. What I remember the most about this book . . . wasn't just the story of the loss that was encountered by the authors but their wisdom in helping others see ways to go on with their lives and not be full of such engulfing sadness. I will always be grateful that this book found me and helped reach such a deeply hurting area in my life."

Natalie, AZ

"The authors have done an excellent job of covering a topic that has not received the attention it deserves. As a grief counselor I frequently interact with mourners who are struggling to adjust to the sudden death of a loved one. I use this book in my sessions and many of my clients read it as part of their grief work. The book is written in plain language and comes across as conversational."

J.D. Ferrara, FL

"My seventeen-year-old son, Roman, died in the prime of life and I didn't have a chance to say goodbye. I found the book to be more than a reference, or quick handling of the matter, I identified with similar emotions, the kick in stomach when you are already emptied of air, and the loss of "clean" closure. This book offered perspectives and "normal" responses and actions for each stage of loss. It identifies and provides descriptions for your recognition and insight. I wanted to read every word, I felt we were joined, in a lot of ways, in our losses and I wanted the insight. The book is organized for easy handling and easy reading. You benefit from the experiences of the writers as they each experienced losses in their lives, and due to their losses, I find myself more apt to believe what they are writing about. If you have experienced loss, you need a book that gives you information and is readable at the same time. This book is it."

C. Slabach, WI

I Wasn't Ready to Say Goodbye

WORKBOOK

UPDATED EDITION

also by Brook Noel and Pamela D. Blair, PhD

*You're Not Alone: Resources and Support for Those
Who Are Grieving*

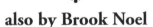

Living with Grief: A Guide to the First Year of Grieving

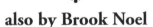

I Wasn't Ready to Say Goodbye Workbook: A Companion Workbook for Surviving, Coping, and Healing After the Sudden Loss of a Loved One

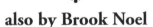

also by Brook Noel

The Change Your Life Challenge: Step-by-Step Solutions for Finding Balance, Creating Contentment, Getting Organized, and Building the Life You Want

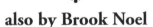

Grief Steps: 10 Steps to Rebuild After the Loss of a Loved One

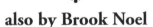

Grief Steps Workbook: 10 Steps to Regroup, Rebuild, and Renew after Any Life Loss

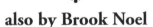

*The Single Parent Resource: An A-Z Manual for the Challenges
of Single Parenting*

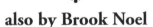

*Surviving Holidays, Birthdays and Special Occasions in the
Grief Journey*

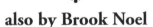

Understanding the Emotional and Physical Effects of Grief

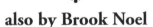

also by Pamela D. Blair, PhD

The Next Fifty Years: A Guide for Women at Mid-Life and Beyond

I Wasn't Ready to Say Goodbye

*a companion workbook for surviving, coping, and
healing after the sudden death of a loved one*

WORKBOOK

UPDATED EDITION

BROOK NOEL AND PAMELA D. BLAIR, PhD

SOURCEBOOKS, INC.
NAPERVILLE, ILLINOIS

Published by Sourcebooks, Inc.
P.O. Box 4410, Naperville, Illinois 60567–4410
(630) 961–3900
Fax: (630) 961–2168
www.sourcebooks.com

Originally published in 2003 by Champion Books, Ltd.

Printed and bound in the United States of America.

POD 10 9 8 7 6 5 4

For George, who taught me how to let go
And for Steve who taught me how to love again.
—*Pamela D Blair*

For 'Samson' who taught me that friendship goes beyond human dimensions,
and for Caleb who taught me that love and kinship go beyond earthly dimensions.
—*Brook Noel*

ACKNOWLEDGMENTS

Pamela D. Blair . . .

Thanks so much to Dr. Charlotte Tomaino, Kathy Murphy, and to everyone in the TBI group. To Gary Leistico, Patricia Ellen, Alyce Branum, Carl and Wilma Machover, and Delores Paddie and Keri for their inspiration. To my children, Aimee, Ian, and Rachel for their contributions. To my husband, Steve, with all my heart I thank you for believing in me. My sister, Marilyn Houston, for her constant support and input to this book. A great big thank you and hug to my clients who inspired me, and to all those close to me who helped me through a very trying time. Brook Noel, fellow writer and spiritual journeyer, I thank you for your vision, talent, and perseverance in seeing this work from its inception to its completion.

And finally, to all those seen and unseen who have been instrumental in this book.

Brook Noel . . .

The first edition of this book was a rather lonely process from concept through publication. I am greatful to have found a compassionate, caring, talented, and thoughtful team in Sourcebooks this second time around. You are all wonderful. A special thanks to Dominique, Barb, Peter, and Todd for their dedication and time to make this journey a reality. To my editor, Shana, thank you for your patience, respect, kind words, and wisdom throughout this process. You are everything I hoped an editor would be.

To Sara Pattow, thank you for being an anchor in my life. As was true in 1997 and now in 2007 your friendship will always be cherished as one of my life's richest treasures. To Mary Ann Klotz, thank you for standing by me and walking me through my darkest nights. To all of Caleb's friends—especially Rob, Steve, and Jeremy—thank you for standing by and becoming a part of our family. To Pamela D. Blair—I feel fortunate to have found you and for your guidance, help, input, support, and partnership throughout the walk of grief and the evolutions of this book.

To my family: Andy, thank you for standing by me through the good times and the bad and providing a steady hand when my world was crumbling. To Sammy . . . a decade ago when I worked on the first edition you were my little angel reminding me daily of life's beauties. You have become even more of an angel with the years and remain my greatest joy in life. And for my Mother, thank you for your support and love through my trials and triumphs. You are the absolute best. I love you with all my heart and soul.

Do not stand
at my grave and weep
I am not there,
I do not sleep.

I am a thousand
winds that blow.
I am the diamond
glints on snow.

I am the sunlight
On the ripened grain.
I am the gentle
Autumn's rain.

When you awaken
in the morning hush,
I am the swift uplifting rush
of quiet birds in
circled flight.
I am the soft stars
that shine at night.

Do not stand
at my grave and cry.
I am not there.
I did not die.

—Hopi Prayer

CONTENTS

Chapter One
Our Stories

"What we call the beginning is often the end.
To make an end is to make a beginning.
The end is where we start from."
—*T.S. Eliot*

Pam's Story

I believe no matter how much pain we're in, there is something inside of us stronger than the pain. That something allows survivors of the worst tragedies to want to live and tell their stories. You can see it in the eyes of someone who has managed to hang on to their dignity in the midst of adversity. It's a kind of stubbornness. You can call it God, the soul, or the human spirit. It is found only when we have been oppressed, or broken, or abandoned, and we remain the one who holds onto what's left. It is this inner something that has allowed me to go on in the face of tremendous loss.

I remember all the vivid, surrealistic details of that morning. The smell of fresh ground coffee brewing lingered in the air as I came to consciousness. I was trying to squeeze one or two more minutes out of my warm bed and feather pillow when the phone rang. Grabbing at the intrusive noise, I put the receiver to my ear and heard nothing but the sound of someone trying to catch her breath. I thought it might be one of those weird "breather" calls until I heard LeAnne say, "Pam, George is in a coma . . . *(long pause)* . . . he had a hemorrhage or something." I felt the molecules in the air begin to thicken as I tried to take a breath so I could talk to George's younger sister. "LeAnne, where are you? What do you mean? I just saw George yesterday afternoon. He looked fine!"

Crying and gasping for air, she replied in a thin voice, "You and Ian have to come here—to the hospital. I think it's important that you bring Ian here now." I tried to remain rational as I remembered that Ian, my twelve-year-old son with George, was getting ready to bolt down the stairs on his way to school. I still needed to pack his lunch box. I thought, *Why is LeAnne bothering me with this? I'm sure it's just nothing. After all, George is young and healthy (and handsome). Comas don't happen to people like him. They don't happen to people I know.*

"LeAnne, why don't we wait and see. He'll probably come to. And besides, Ian is just about to leave for school and he has a test today. Why don't you call back in a few minutes after you have more information and I'll bring him down to the hospital later. It's probably not as bad as . . ." She interrupted my rambling with a bold, deliberate, almost cold intonation in her voice. "*Now.* You have to come now. It's really bad. There's a lot of blood in his brain and he probably won't live."

Blood in his brain. I sat down hard. What was I hearing? Was I hearing that George, the man I had loved as my husband and the father of my child, and who had become a dear friend and loving co-parent after our divorce, was about to leave the earth? Come on. People exaggerate. LeAnne is exaggerating. After all, George means as much to her as he does to me, and his son Ian, and his once stepdaughter, Aimee.

"Okay, LeAnne, I'll take the day off from work and I'll bring Ian to the hospital. Where are you?"

She replied in an almost inaudible voice, "The emergency room. I'll meet you there."

My limbs were numb, the blood was gone from my face and neck, and I wasn't sure I could make my mouth work. Steve, my husband of seven years, had left for his office in the city, and I was alone. I would have to tell Ian myself. I would have to tell Ian that the dad who loved to be with him on weekends, who lived for his son's little league games and karate matches, was probably brain dead. I would have to tell my daughter, Aimee. Part of me thought that if I could just see George and tell him loudly how much his son needed him, he wouldn't slip away into death's darkness. That's it. I would scream at him and bring him back to us.

Somehow I made my legs work. One numb foot in front of the other. At the bottom of the stairs I called, "Ian, meet me in my bedroom. I have something to tell you." I kept telling myself, *You will remain calm . . . think logically . . . don't upset the boy too much, just keep calm.*

How do you describe this strange limbo moment where life slows down and everything around you falls away into unimportance? It felt like there was no house with its comfortable furniture around me, no more smell of coffee, no cat rubbing my legs for attention, no appointments on the calendar— all that existed for now were the two small, round, brown eyes of my little boy resting on mine.

I told Ian what little I knew. There, sitting on the edge of my now neatly made bed, he melted into tears. Deep sobs and a lot of "How did this happen? What happened to him?" over and over again. His voice was cracking, rising and falling, the way twelve-year-old boy's voices sometimes do. I comforted him. I knew that was my only role, comforter to my son with no one to comfort me.

I called my daughter, Aimee, George's stepdaughter, nine months pregnant with her first child. She agreed to join us. We made our way to the hospital, not talking. Ian looked out the car window and I could tell he wondered why everyone driving past us looked so normal, so unaffected by our plight. Didn't they know what was going on? How could they go about their business knowing George was dying *or dead?* Why are they behaving as if nothing happened? I felt as if I were moving through someone else's movie. Everything felt surreal, in slow motion.

No human being is without feelings. From a baby's first cry to a dying person's last look at friends and family, our primary response to the world around us is colored by emotion. Whether that world seems to us friendly or frightening, beautiful or ugly, pleasant or disagreeable, affects the way we approach others, and indeed influences everything we do. I do not believe that such feelings arise in us solely due to environmental conditions, or to genetic factors, however important these both may be. Members of the same family, placed in the same kinds of situations, react in very different ways. Our emotions are a conscious response to our experience, but they are self-generated and reveal something important about our character.

It felt like I had no emotions and no character that day. I was skin and bones and brain and blood vessels making attempts at movement. Lips in slow motion on a frozen face with unfamiliar arms and legs, a mind repeating over and over, *this is crazy, this is crazy.* George's mother and sister waited with Ian, Aimee, and me in the emergency room. We all looked the same as we did last week, only now we were more robot-like, sitting and standing and walking and pacing around a room with hard plastic chairs and a TV set hanging from the ceiling. I couldn't look at George's mom with her soft round face and gray hair. A gentle lady of sixty-two with kind blue eyes—the same kind blue eyes that George had. If I looked at her I would have seen the pain. The pain of a woman who was told she would probably never have children and to whom George was a miracle, a gift from God—her first-born.

To me, the emotions are "real" in the sense that I can perceive them objectively as a luminous atmosphere surrounding every living being. Every time we feel an emotion, there is a discharge of energy in the emotional field, whether slight or strong, and this produces a characteristic vibration and a color—the "footprint" of that particular emotion. I could "see" the emotion in the room.

George was brain dead. The doctor said he had suffered a massive cerebral aneurysm. He was dead and he looked like he was sleeping—the machines kept his lungs rising and falling, his heart beating, his face a rosy healthy glow. I encouraged Ian to hold his hand, to say goodbye. He was brave. He did. He cried and said, "Goodbye, Daddy, I love you." Aimee took her private moment with him also. George had, only the week before, stopped by to visit her in her new apartment, to place his hand on her baby-full belly, to say congratulations.

George's wife said I could have some time alone with him. Because I believe that people in comas can "hear," I told him "thank you for our son and for the love you showed Aimee. Thank you for the time we had together." I think he heard me, if not with his ears, with his soul. I asked him to please be an angel in our son's life—to watch over him. The hospital staff began disconnecting the machines as the family encircled the hospital bed, holding hands, and praying.

I tell my story because I believe in the power of story to heal. As a therapist and workshop leader, I find it rewarding to help others tell their story. The stories I hear about loss are as diverse as fingerprints—each one slightly different from the next. And yet, when we gather like we did at a recent workshop I conducted, the attendees share and the connection to each other is immediate and profound. Regardless of where we are in the process of loss, we become supportive as we relate and recognize each other's pain. A sense of community and acceptance is vital to our spiritual and emotional healing.

In her book, *The Fruitful Darkness,* Buddhist anthropologist and depth psychologist Joan Halifax reflects on our collective as well as personal stories when she writes, "stories are our protectors, like our immune system, defending against attacks of debilitating alienation . . . They are the connective tissue between culture and nature, self and other, life and death, that sew the worlds together, and in telling, the soul quickens and comes alive."

In his classic book, *Reaching Out,* Henri Nouwen writes that though our own story "can be hard to tell, full of disappointments and frustrations, deviations and stagnations . . . it is the only story we have and there will be no hope for the future when the past remains unconfessed, unreceived, and misunderstood."

Hopefully, the stories and information in this book will help you feel less alone as you struggle to find the path that will lead you across rivers of grief and through forests of sadness. We hope in some small way that we can be your support network and a touchstone for sanity during a very difficult time.

Brook's Story

It was a day in October that changed my perception of life, and my perception of death, forever. It was the day I lost my brother, who was not only a brother, but in many ways a father, a friend, and a lifeline.

The day was unseasonably warm for a Wisconsin October. It was the fourth of the month and the thermometer showed a temperature near seventy degrees. With weather like that, no Wisconsinite would stay indoors. My husband, daughter, and I decided to take a trip to Manitowoc, a town about an hour north of our then-home-base in the Milwaukee suburbs. Manitowoc housed a Maritime Museum that we had yet to visit. The main feature was a submarine, complete with tour. That afternoon we walked the streets, looked in the shops, took the tour, and bought our two-and-a-half-year-old daughter a blue hat, which read *U.S.S. Cobia*. Our daughter posed with the hat, her smile radiating happiness.

We left Manitowoc around five that evening to return home. A dear friend of mine had traveled into town and we had planned to meet at six for dinner. I glanced at my watch as we continued the drive, knowing I would be a few minutes late. We had planned that she would leave a message with her restaurant choice and I would meet her. We arrived home a bit after six. My neighbors, Kevin and Mary Ann, were outside barbecuing. I stopped over briefly to say hello and let Samantha show off her new hat. I apologized for my quick departure and ducked into the house to check messages and find out where Sara had chosen for dinner.

The red digital display showed four messages. I hit play. The first was from my mother. Five simple words, "Brook—call me right away." The second was from Sara, with the name of the restaurant. The third was from my mother again, this time her voice thick with a tone I couldn't discern. "Brook you *must* call me right away. There has been a terrible accident." I immediately pushed stop on the machine and dialed my mother's number. Both my brother and mother continued to live in the town where I was raised. It's a small resort town called Manitowish Waters, about five hours north of my then-Milwaukee home. Life is simple there. You work; you ski; you enjoy the woods, the lakes; you watch the Packers and enjoy the seasons as they unfold. Outsiders make great attempts to vacation there. Often the north woods has been dubbed "God's Country," and life is full and fun there.

My mother answered on the first ring. I can still hear our voices to this day and picture myself standing beneath the archway of our guest bedroom. "Mom, it's me. What's up?" I asked inquisitively, never prepared for the two-word response that would vibrate over the phone.

"Caleb's dead."

Immediately my knees gave out and I shouted "No," before falling to the floor, the questions, the disbelief, lingering around me. I asked how, but did not hear the reply. I crawled into the guest bed with the cordless phone pushed to my ear and curled my body into a tight ball. My daughter had walked up from behind and was patting me gently on the back. "It's all right Mama," said the innocent two-year-old voice. "It's all right Mama." Andy, my husband, came to take Samantha from the room and I simply mouthed the two words my mother had spoken: *Caleb's dead*.

Still on the line, my mother was talking and crying and I couldn't unscramble the words. I remember only one sentence, "Brook is Andy there? You need to hang up the phone and call me back. Have Andy call me back." I set down the phone still writhing on the bed, wanting desperately to escape the unwelcome reality that had suddenly become claustrophobic. Rising, I walked into the living room. I looked briefly at my daughter and Andy, before running from the house. The points thereafter are somewhat vague and gathered from what I've been told of my response.

I entered into my neighbor's kitchen and fell into her arms as I told her the news. She quickly took me outside and huddled me close. She held me on the wooden steps as I stared at the cement and she whispered, "You are in shock. Try and breathe. Don't talk." I remember my hands and body trembling violently. "Look at my hands," I whispered, "What happened to my hands?" I watched them jump from left to right, operating independently of my mind. Her words soothed me from some otherworld. "You are in shock. Try and breathe." MaryAnn's husband, Kevin, went to my house and took Samantha back to have dinner with their family. With Samantha out of the house, MaryAnn escorted me back home to Andy where the two of them called my mother.

The details unfurled. Caleb and his faithful chocolate lab, Samson, had been duck hunting on a marsh with three friends. They had rowed a boat out about twenty minutes to the site that was thought to have the best potential. While waiting for the official opening time, Caleb was eyeing some geese flying overhead. At that moment he was stung by a yellow jacket just over his eyebrow. Within minutes, Caleb would go unconscious. His friends performed CPR as they frantically rowed back to shore. Unable to fit in the boat, his faithful dog swam across the marsh, unwilling to leave his master. His friends broke into his truck, using his cellular phone to call the paramedics. The local paramedics arrived and were then intercepted by a special team sent from the hospital twenty-five miles away.

Despite the efforts of friends, paramedics and doctors, Caleb never came to nor responded to Epinephrine or any other drug. My mother was told he had suffered a fatal, profound, anaphylactic shock reaction to the sting of a bee. Caleb had been stung by bees before and never had anything more than a mild reaction. We, nor he, even knew of this bee allergy.

My brother was a strong and vital young man. He owned a successful printing shop, which he built from the ground up. He was a National Barefoot Water-ski Champion who was in great physical health and a prime athlete. He was about 200 pounds, and in one day, we had to come to understand that a bee, no bigger than an inch, had taken the life from this handsome twenty-seven-year-old man. It is something that I think we all are still trying to comprehend. It is something that I don't think we ever fully will, but we each must find our own way to cope and go on successfully—that is the best tribute we can give to this great man who touched our lives.

When Caleb died, I looked for someone to hold my hand and to understand what I was feeling. I wasn't ready for a support group; all I wanted to do was to curl up in my bed, hide from the world, and have something or someone convince me it would, someday, be all right again. I scanned bookstores looking for something I could relate to but found very little coverage on sudden death. The other books didn't understand the unique challenges of facing a death in this way. Eventually, I gave up the search for that book.

As time has passed, I have learned more about what I have endured and what I have to endure to move on with my life. I have spoken with others—some in the recent aftermath of loss and some who lost someone tragically years ago—many of whom are looking for guidance similar to what I had searched for. With these people in mind, I decided to create the book I wish would have been there for me. I met my coauthor, Pam, while working on a book entitled *The Single Parent Resource.* There was an immediate closeness between the two of us, even though we lived two thousand miles apart. When I decided to write this book, I felt compelled to call her and see if she would consider writing the book with me. Fate must have nudged me to call, since at that point, I didn't know she had experienced sudden loss in her life as well.

We cannot offer you any quick fixes. We cannot give you a tidy outline that will divide grief recovery into a neat and precise process or stages. We cannot tell you that six months from now the world will be back in alignment. We have seen too much to offer such hollow promises. What we can promise is that in these pages we will do our best to offer you a hand to hold and words to guide you through this unfamiliar maze moving toward emerging on the other side.

Sudden Loss Comes Again

Brook's Story . . . February 2005

It was a Sunday morning much like any other. The Wisconsin weather was cold and brittle while I was warm and cozy in my home with my daughter and husband. The ringing of the phone interrupted our family moment. Most would say the ring sounded like it always had, but I heard it echo through the hallway—issuing a warning to the answerer. My father, age sixty-one, had entered a hospital while traveling abroad in Trinidad. In an all-too-short three-week span he was diagnosed and died from advanced colon cancer, unable to reach a condition that was stable enough for me to bring him back to the United States.

Although well-versed by now in grief, the road before me was still unfamiliar.

I found myself grieving not only my dad, but my brother—even harder than I had the first time.

As I waded through this maze with grief both new and old, I kept a list of the lessons I learned along the way and will hold with me always. I share these with you in hopes they offer comfort in your journey.

I learned that sometimes "not knowing" is the only thing to know.

I learned that sometimes it's okay to forget everything and just sleep for ten or twenty hours.

I learned I have a lot more to learn about myself.

I learned that the answers we often look for outside of ourselves, can only be found within.

I learned that I can blame anything and everything until I run out of breath—but I become empowered when I quit asking, "why me?" and start asking, "what will I do with this?"

I learned that there is nothing as precious as right now—even when "now" doesn't seem precious.

I learned that I cannot make up for today by living or working "harder" or "doing more" or "being healthier" or "spending more time" tomorrow.

I learned that I can never know what the day may bring, but it is up to me at its close, to know what the day brought.

I re-learned the value of a moment.

Chapter Two
The First Few Weeks

SUGGESTED READING:

I Wasn't Ready to Say Goodbye
Chapter 2: Notes for the First Few Weeks

"And people answered the phone for me.
And people cooked for me.
And people understood for me.
My dearest friends cared for me
when I didn't care."
—*Wendy Feiereisen*

At this moment, in the direct aftermath of losing someone tragically, there is so little anyone can say. We cannot find the words to offer you peace—though we wish it were a gift we could give you. We promise you now that we will give you everything we can to help you make your way through this. We will help you wind a path through the haze, the confusion, and the pain that is gripping at your core.

For the first few weeks, do not concern yourself with what you will do, where you will go, or what lies in the future. For now, we ask that you simply follow the guidelines in this chapter. There will be time to cope, to understand, to process—later. Right now, you simply need to take care of *you*.

Treat Yourself as If You Were in Intensive Care

You are in the process of going through one of the most traumatic experiences a person can endure. The challenges you have already faced, both physically and mentally, will leave you vulnerable, exhausted, and weak. It is imperative that you focus directly on yourself and on any dependents. Find ways to get your needs met first in these few weeks.

In the first week or so you will probably feel stunned and overwhelmed. You may also feel numb or hysterical. Your emotional system shuts down, providing temporary insulation from the full impact of your loss. You will go through the motions; it will look like you're coping well sometimes.

In her book, *The Worst Loss*, Barbara D. Rosof writes, "In shock you may be unable to move or speak coherently; people report that they cannot think. Shock responses may also be active and intense; you may have screamed, or run from the room, or physically attacked the bringer of the news. All of these behaviors are means of shutting down, or distancing yourself from a reality that you do not yet have a way to deal with. As you look back, your behavior may seem bizarre and totally out of character for you. Remember that your entire world had been knocked out from under you. You were in free fall, and your first task was to find any way to stop the fall."

When the funeral is over and your relatives and friends have gone home, the shock begins to wear off. It is important not to make any decisions that will have a lasting impact on your life for example, sell the house, give away the person's belongings, etc.) while you are in shock.

Your Immediate Needs

Children

Who can help care for your children? Even when you are present, you will likely be occupied with your own grief. This is perfectly normal. Do not try to "do it all". Instead, create a list of people who can help by being present to offer additional support to your children.

Monday	Support Person	Phone Number
Tuesday	Support Person	Phone Number
Wednesday	Support Person	Phone Number
Thursday	Support Person	Phone Number
Friday	Support Person	Phone Number
Saturday	Support Person	Phone Number
Sunday	Support Person	Phone Number

Are there any other support people available that your children should know about?

_____

_____

_____

_____

_____

_____

_____

_____

Your Support System
Who can you call if you need support or assistance?

_____

_____

_____

_____

_____

_____

_____

School and Work

Has your employer been contacted and notified of any time you will need away from work?

Manager's Name   **Manager's Direct Number**

_____

Employer's Name   **Employer's Number**

_____

Has your child's school been contacted and notified of any time needed away from school, or any special assistance needed for other children?

Name of principle, teacher, or director   **Direct Line**

_____

School's Name   **School's Number**

_____

* Have a friend help make these calls if you are not up to it.

Are there any urgent or pressing bills or claims that need to be filed in the next couple of weeks?

❑ Mortgage or Rent   Contact Information _____
❑ Other Loan Payments   Contact Information _____
❑ Insurance   Contact Information _____
❑ Car Payments   Contact Information _____
❑ Life Insurance   Contact Information _____
❑ Accounts Payable   Contact Information _____
❑ CCD'S   Contact Information _____
❑ Taxes   Contact Information _____
❑ Other   Contact Information _____
❑ Other   Contact Information _____
❑ Other   Contact Information _____

A Checklist of Calls to Make

Below you will find other calls that need to be made. Let your support people help or make these calls for you. Discuss them with your support person before they call. If this list is overwhelming at the moment, come back to it later or let your support team bring relevant calls to your attention.

❑ Call a support person to help you. Give the support person this list and let them work through it and ask questions as necessary.

❑ Choose a funeral home to assist in arrangements. Set date and time for funeral and memorial services. (See worksheet on page 21).
Funeral Home Name _____ Phone Number _____
Contact Person _____

❑ Contact the newspaper for the obituary.

❑ Choose a memorial or charity for any gifts or donations. Ask family members and friends of your loved one what ideas and groups they would suggest. Request more information from any groups you would like to learn more about.
Selected Group _____
Contact Information _____
_____

Depending upon your relationship to the deceased, you may need to also make the following calls:

❑ Notify all insurance companies—social security, credit union, trade union, fraternal, military, standard life, credit card, etc. Check for income from any of these sources as well.

❑ Call all debtors in a timely manner. Insurance may cancel out some debts. For other debts, ask for a payment plan. Notarized copies of the death certificate are usually required, it is best to have several on hand for these circumstances.

❑ If the deceased lived alone, contact the landlord and utilities. Select a group of people to help move the deceased's belongings from the apartment/home.

❑ Contact a lawyer and the executor of the will, if a will is in place. If there is no will, contact a lawyer for guidance.

Who Needs to Be Notified

Make a list of people who need to be notified. Try to obtain the deceased's address book or cell phone for phone numbers and people who might otherwise be overlooked. You may also choose to share this page with friends and other family members. They may have other useful suggestions.

Contacted	Name	Phone Number

Call Log

If the person who has died is of your immediate family, you will be receiving many phone calls, visitors, and cards. Have a friend come by to take messages, answer the door, and answer the phone. Most callers do not expect to speak directly with the family but simply wish to express their condolences. Have someone log your incoming calls on the log below. You can return them if you like, although don't feel obligated to do so.

Name and Phone Number	Message

Delivering a Eulogy

You may use this worksheet to create a eulogy or provide it to the person whom you would like to deliver the eulogy. According to Terence B. Foley and Amanda Bennett (*In Memoriam,* Simon & Schuster, 1997), "The most important thing to remember when delivering a eulogy is that it is a gift. A gift for you to be able to speak about a family member or friend before those who also loved and respected him . . . It is not a performance, nor will it be judged as such. Your job is to be thoughtful and genuine . . . "

This form should get you thinking about those things that were most important about the deceased. As you deliver the eulogy, do not rush, take your time. If you decide to use humor, make sure it is done with affection. Avoid jokes and stories that would embarrass those present. If you lose your composure, give yourself a moment of quiet, take a deep breath or a drink of water, and go on.

My relationship with the deceased:

_____

_____

I've known him/her for how long:

_____

_____

How we met:

_____

_____

_____

_____

_____

_____

What I remember most . . .

_____

_____

_____

_____

Positive qualities:

_____

_____

_____

_____

What was eccentric about them (presented with affection):

_____

_____

_____

_____

Kindnesses I received from the deceased:

_____

_____

_____

_____

_____

What would the deceased say about the events today:

_____

_____

_____

_____

_____

Integrating what we learned from this person into our own lives is a constant memorial and source of comfort for the family. Therefore, consider the following three questions:

What did I learn from this person (through example or teaching):

_____

_____

_____

_____

_____

How do I plan to implement what I learned from them:

_____

_____

_____

_____

_____

What words of wisdom would the deceased want us to remember:

_____

_____

_____

_____

_____

NOTES:

_____

_____

_____

_____

_____

When honoring a loved one, go with what feels intuitively right to you. What touches you deeply will likely touch others. When Brook was in her teens, she lost a friend in a car accident. At the service, the friend's father got up to speak. Barely able to get the words out between gasps and tears, he delivered a few minutes that moved everyone in the room. The deceased was a performer and he ended his talk with, "Always a performer, let's give him one more standing ovation for the time he gave us." Everyone in the room stood, clapping with all their might, tears streaming down their faces as they honored their friend. Typical? No. But it moved everyone more than any other spoken words could have.

Naturally, the best way to honor a friend is to speak from the heart—your heart. What you say doesn't have to be eloquent or full of fancy epitaphs. Simple, straightforward, and heartfelt words are what the family is longing to hear. Again, there is really no right or wrong way to eulogize a friend. You can sing a song, write a poem, dance a dance, or read what someone else has written. Use your imagination and trust your instincts. If you are intuitively drawn to a particular reading or creative act, it may even be your friend who is gently nudging you, instructing you on how to celebrate his life.

NOTES:

20

The Memorial Service

When the person in charge of the memorial service does not know the deceased, consider filling out this form, and giving it to them. Keep a copy for yourself. The information included on the form will be an aid in creating a meaningful service. The form will also be useful if the person in charge knew your loved one.

If at all possible, do not fill out this form alone. Ask friends and family to contribute information. If your loved one had a career, chances are they have a resume in a file somewhere. Their resume may help fill in some of the blanks.

INFORMATION TO PROVIDE TO THE PERSON (OR CLERGYPERSON) IN CHARGE:

Name of deceased: _____ Age: _____

Cause of death: _____ Date of birth: _____

Religious background (if any): _____ Date of death: _____

Type of service the deceased would have liked (i.e. quiet, casual, formal, offbeat): _____

Those who would like to participate: _____

Family background: _____

Education: _____

Career (or career aspirations): _____

Club memberships or affiliations: _____

Activities or hobbies: _____

Relationships: _____

What kind of books did they read? _____

What were their dreams? _____

What were they most proud of? _____

Who were their friends, family? _____

What kind of music did they enjoy? _____

Favorite bible verse or inspirational verse:

Favorite poet or poems:

Favorite charity/charities:

NOTES:

_____

_____

_____

_____

_____

_____

_____

_____

_____

_____

_____

_____

_____

_____

_____

_____

What to Expect: Physical and Emotional Changes

Fear and anxiety increase when we face the unknown. When we understand that we are traveling a path others have traveled and survived, our fear and anxiety often lessen. Below, we have listed common physical and emotional effects encountered on the grief journey. You may experience some or all of these feelings and symptoms. When you feel them, realize they are normal. You are not going crazy. You are not alone. This is part of the process. Instead of worrying or obsessing about these "side effects" honor them as signs to slow down and listen to your body.

Chest pain	Restlessness	Sleep difficulties
Dry mouth	Crying	Exhaustion
Weakness	Dizziness	Numbness
Shakiness	Disorientation	Listlessness
Migraines or headaches	Upset stomach	Heart palpitations
Anxiety	Poor appetite	Overeating
Social avoidance	Shortness of breath	Aches and Pains

What prompts is your body giving you to slow down? What are some ways you could honor those prompts? (Example: Take a few minutes to sit down and breathe deeply. Take a nap.)

_____

_____

_____

_____

_____

_____

_____

Important: If any of the conditions listed above are troublesome or concern you, or persist relentlessly, contact your doctor or a medial professional for their recommendation.

The Power of Friends

If possible, choose a close friend to keep near you through the first week or two. Let this person help you make decisions, hear your fears or concerns, and be the shoulder for you to lean on. Give them a copy of this book. Later, as you move through the grieving process, it will be very helpful to have someone who has "been there" and understands what you are talking about thoroughly.

Our energy is so depleted in the first few weeks after loss, it's hard to even ask for help. We have included a handout on the next page that can be photocopied freely and given to your inner circle of friends and relatives. You may be reluctant to do this, but please do. Even when we don't think we need people right now, we do indeed.

The following two entries summarize beautifully what those who face grief need from the people around them:

> "I'll cry with you,'
> she whispered
> "until we run out of tears.
> Even if it's forever.
> We'll do it together."
> There it was . . . a simple
> promise of connection.
> The loving alliance of
> grief and hope that
> blesses both our breaking
> apart and our coming
> together again.
> Molly Fumia, *Safe Passage*

"Needed: A strong, deep person wise enough to allow me to grieve in the depth of who I am, and strong enough to hear my pain without turning away.

I need someone who believes that the sun will rise again, but who does not fear my darkness. Someone who can point out the rocks in my way without making me a child by carrying me. Someone who can stand in thunder and watch the lightning and believe in a rainbow." Fr. Joe Mahoney, *Concerns of Police Survivors Newsletter*

(This is excerpted from a beautiful book on grief titled *Forever Remembered: Cherished Messages of Hope, Love, and Comfort from Courageous People Who Have Lost a Loved One.* Compendium Publishing.)

Understanding Our Support Needs

Reaching out to others for help is difficult, especially when we are at an emotional low and our energy is at a premium. Yet it remains vital to identify the support that we need in our lives. In the chart below, write down each specific support need in the first column. In the next column, write down who can give you that support. Once you have completed your chart, make an action plan to contact the people in column two to get the support that will help you heal.

WHAT TYPE OF SUPPORT I NEED	WHO CAN GIVE ME THAT SUPPORT
Talking / Communication	
Physical tasks / Self-care	
Financial needs	
Day-to-day life management	
Professional or group support	

A Guide for Those Helping Others with Grief
(photocopy and give to close friends and loved ones)

Don't try to find the magic words or formula to eliminate the pain. Nothing can erase or minimize the painful tragedy your friend or loved one is facing. Your primary role at this time is simply to "be there." Don't worry about what to say or do, just be a presence that the person can lean on when needed.

Don't try to minimize or make the person feel better. When we care about someone, we hate to see them in pain. Often we'll say things like, "I know how you feel," or "perhaps, it was for the best," in order to minimize their hurt. While this can work in some instances, it never works with grief.

Help with responsibilities. Even though a life has stopped, life doesn't. One of the best ways to help is to run errands, prepare food, take care of the kids, do laundry, and help with the simplest of maintenance.

Don't expect the person to reach out to you. Many people say, "call me if there is anything I can do." At this stage, the person who is grieving will be overwhelmed at the simple thought of picking up a phone. If you are close to this person, simply stop over, and begin to help. People need this but don't think to ask. There are many people who will be with you during the good times—but few that are there in life's darkest hour.

Talk through decisions. While working through the grief process, many bereaved people report difficulty with decision making. Be a sounding board for your friend or loved one and help them think through decisions.

Don't be afraid to say the name of the deceased. Those who have lost someone usually speak of them often, and believe it or not, need to hear the deceased's name and stories. In fact, many grievers welcome this.

Excerpted from "I Wasn't Ready to Say Goodbye: a guide for surviving, coping, and healing after the sudden death of a loved one" by Brook Noel and Pamela D. Blair, PhD (Champion Press, 2000)

Remember that time does not heal all wounds. Your friend or loved one will change because of what has happened. Everyone grieves differently. Some will be "fine" and then experience their true grief a year later, others grieve immediately. There are no timetables, no rules—be patient.

Remind the bereaved to take care of themselves. Eating, resting, and self-care are all difficult tasks when besieged by the taxing emotions of grief. You can help by keeping the house stocked with healthy foods that are already prepared or easy to prepare. Help with the laundry. Take over some errands so the bereaved can rest. However, do not push the bereaved to do things they may not be ready for. Many grievers say, "I wish they would just follow my lead." While it may be upsetting to see the bereaved withdrawing from people and activities—it is normal. They will rejoin as they are ready.

Avoid judging. Don't tell the person how to react or handle their emotions or situation. Simply let him/her know that you support their decisions and will help in any way possible.

Share a Meal. Since meal times can be especially lonely, invite the bereaved over regularly to share a meal, or take a meal to their home. Consider inviting the bereaved out on important dates like the one-month anniversary of the death, the deceased's birthday, etc.

Make a list of everything that needs to be done with the bereaved. This could include everything from bill paying to plant watering. Prioritize these by importance. Help the bereaved complete as many tasks as possible. If there are many responsibilities, find one or more additional friends to support you.

Make a personal commitment to help the one grieving get through this. After a death, many friendships change or disintegrate. People don't know how to relate to the one who is grieving, or they get tired of being around someone who is sad. Vow to see your friend or loved one through this, to be their anchor in their darkest hour.

Excerpted from "I Wasn't Ready to Say Goodbye: a guide for surviving, coping, and healing after the sudden death of a loved one" by Brook Noel and Pamela D. Blair, PhD (Sourcebooks, 2008)

Chapter Three
Difficult Emotions

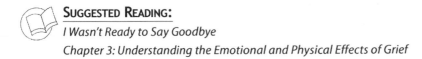

SUGGESTED READING:
I Wasn't Ready to Say Goodbye
Chapter 3: Understanding the Emotional and Physical Effects of Grief

> "When people ask me what I was feeling . . . I didn't know how to respond. I wasn't feeling any one emotion—I was feeling everything—all at the same time."
> —*Anonymous*

At some point in our grief work, we are likely to find ourselves recounting the days with our loved one in our minds. We may also play out different scenarios of the death, trying to understand what has happened. For some, the review completely preoccupies the mind, and despite our wishes we can think of nothing else.

As is the case with post traumatic stress disorder, you may find yourself living and reliving the experiences you had with your loved one during the days, hours or minutes just before the death occurred. "If only I had not taken that road . . . If only I had said 'don't go' . . . If only I had been there I might have prevented the accident . . ." and on and on.

As you read this, what "if onlys" enter your mind?

_____

_____

_____

_____

For each "if only" statement, write a realistic statement to balance it.

_____

_____

_____

_____

_____

_____

With the first news of loss, our mind acts as a filter. It immediately sifts through the facts and details, offering only the barest to keep us informed. Too much detail would be more than we could bear. So our mind filters and filters until our bodies and hearts can cope with a little more. At some point, when the body has recovered somewhat, the mind lets larger blocks of information in. At this point, by human instinct, we look for resolution. We struggle to make sense of what has happened and that is where the instant replay begins. We explore every option—even the outlandish. These explorations are what allow us to slowly internalize the fact that life, as we once knew it, has changed.

This is a pivotal point in the grieving process. At this point, or close to it, we are finally acknowledging the death in reality.

The "If Only" Mind Game

"If only" is the game of guilt that plagues many survivors. The "if only" questions surface intensely in cases of unexpected death. The situation is so "out of control" that our human nature fights and searches for a way to control the uncontrollable. As we yearn to make sense of the senseless, often the only route of control we find is to blame ourselves.

"I should have known," or "If only I had talked to him for two minutes longer . . ." are sentiments that those who grieve may say to themselves. Realize this guilt is a way of trying to gain control over the uncontrollable, and then work to let it go. Each time it enters, remember that this is our longing for control, but don't give in to the guilt. You cannot change what has happened and odds are you couldn't have changed it beforehand. No one knows these things are going to happen—no one has that much control or foresight. Brook found that she ran on the "I should've known" treadmill.

Anger

Who wouldn't be angry when someone they loved so dearly is suddenly taken from them? Anger is natural in this situation and it is actually a healthy part of the grieving process. Yet anger takes different forms, some of them healthy, and some of them unhealthy.

Let's examine the types of anger that are natural, though unhealthy. Some of us will express anger when we are not getting the support we need from friends, family, or work. While intensely wrapped in our grief, we usually don't think to ask for support. Instead we lash out at those close to us with hostility, irritability, and anger. If we can recognize this anger for what it is, we can use it in a healthy way. This is a clue that we are not receiving the support we need. We need to ask for more or seek out other support networks.

Displaced anger is simply misdirected anger. We want someone to take responsibility for what has happened. We need someone to blame and to be held accountable. We may scream or yell at those who cared for the person at the hospital. We may become angry with those who were with the person when he died. Displaced anger is completely natural and will lessen as you learn to accept what has happened.

Anger can also surface when we recall past moments or turmoil, pain, or unresolved anger within our relationship with the person we have lost. Suddenly we are forced to realize we will never share another physical interaction with this person. When that happens, memories flood through. Within these memories there are bound to be recollections of feisty exchanges, arguments, and past hurts. Wishing we had more time with the loved one, we may overcriticize ourselves for any time there was conflict in the past. It is unrealistic, however, to expect perfection in any relationship. Immersing ourselves in the "should haves" and "could haves" of the past will only prevent us from dealing effectively with anger in the present.

What "should haves" and "could haves" do you recite to yourself?

Why Am I Angry?

Our anger often stems from feeling something unjust or preventable has occurred. We might feel that we could have done something differently, and thus direct our anger inward. Or we might feel that those around us should have done something differently, and we direct our anger outward.

What "should haves" and "could haves" do you recite repeatedly to yourself? Include those you feel you personally "should have done" as well as the "should haves" and "could haves" for other people involved in your loss. IMPORTANT: Don't censor your list. If you feel angry about something yet don't want to write it down because it "doesn't make sense" or is "ridiculous"—that is one more reason to write it down. We must get our feelings out in the open in order to deal with them. Try this now by completing the sentences below.

I am angry because I think I (could/should) have . . .	I am angry because I think _____ (could/should) have . . .

Consider talking this list through with a close friend or support group. The past is gone. We cannot control it, and when we continue to run "could and should" scripts, we limit our ability to heal and move forward.

Appropriate anger is the point that we all hope to get to eventually. In this phase, we can take our anger, in whatever form, and vent it. There are many ways to release anger appropriately. Here are a few . . . place a checkmark next to any that you think would be helpful to you. Try one of these exercises the next time you find yourself upset.

❑ beat a pillow

❑ create a sacred space where you can go and not be heard or seen to let the anger out of your system

❑ use journaling to record and release your angry feelings

❑ take a walk out into an unpopulated area and scream until you are exhausted

❑ talk with a friend, therapist, or counselor

❑ have a good cry, let the tears flow

Anger also occurs when we suppress our feelings. Anger is not the most accepted emotion in today's culture. In fact, many people don't even recognize anger as part of the grieving process. Depending on our support network and situation, we may be encouraged not to show our anger. When this happens, the anger still exists and needs to be released, so it is released inward. This can cause a variety of problems. We may become sick, depressed, have chronic pain, or begin having nightmares.

Below, list healthy alternatives for releasing anger.

_____

_____

_____

_____

Anger is especially common with tragic deaths. Since we could do nothing to stop or prevent the loss and are left only to interpret it, we may become frustrated and develop feelings of helplessness. Bouts of crying are the most common release for this anger. It's easy to not release this anger and to turn it inward. If you suspect you may be doing so, talk to a friend or counselor to help release these feelings.

As you look at your grieving process, do you feel you have expressed your anger? If so, how? (Write about it below. Feel free to use another piece of paper if you need more room to write.) If you are having problems identifying your anger, you likely have not faced it yet.

_____

_____

_____

_____

Screaming Exercise

Sometimes the only thing left to do is SCREAM! Emotions may well up inside you and they need a place to go. It can be a release and a relief to scream as loud as you can and to say whatever comes to mind. It will be a challenge to find an appropriate place to do this exercise. You may have to travel some distance to find a wide open space where no one can hear you. Here is an example of how Pam and her sister Marilyn solved the problem:

"A few months after my sister's husband died suddenly and I was still reeling from George's death, we decided to go to Canada to attend a workshop. In our free time we drove across vast empty spaces with miles of road and no one around. We found ourselves in the car one afternoon in the middle of a Canadian "no man's land" highway screaming 'Why did you die!,' 'I hate you for dying,' 'This death stuff really sucks!' and a host of other expletives. We laughed at how ridiculous we sounded and we cried because we needed to. We decided it was safest if the one who wasn't crying drove the car because it's hard to see the road with tears in your eyes!"

Our intense emotions need to have an outlet, otherwise they can make us sick. A very potent outlet for our grief is to go to a private location (your parked car can serve this purpose very well) and SCREAM and RANT as loudly as you can. By giving ourselves permission to do this, we validate ourselves and our healing process. Do not stifle this need to give voice to your pain. It is your right as a human being to express your deepest feelings in this way if you choose to do so.

Record your feelings after completing this exercise.

_____

_____

_____

_____

_____

_____

_____

_____

_____

_____

_____

Fear

Throughout our grief work, fear can be debilitating. Some people experience fear in a small number of areas, while others are overwhelmed by it. It is perfectly natural to be fearful. We have experienced the most unexpected tragedy. Common fears include fearing any situation that remotely resembles how the loved one died, fearing that others we love will be harmed, fearing we will be unable to go on, fearing we will die ourselves, and fearing the simplest activities will lead to tragedy.

Fear serves several purposes. In the initial stages of grief, it gives us something to focus on besides the death that has taken place. It also offers potential control. If we fear that riding in a car could kill us and we choose not to ride in a car, we create the illusion of control. As explained earlier, with tragic death it's common to seek any control we can find. Most of the time, fear will run its course naturally. If you find that you have any fear that is, or is becoming, debilitating, or that manifests itself as panic attacks, talk to a professional.

What do you fear?

_____

_____

_____

_____

Is this fear rational or irrational? _____

Most of our fears are irrational and by writing out the irrationality, we equip ourselves with the strength to fight our fear. How, specifically, is your fear irrational?

_____

_____

_____

_____

The next time your fear surfaces, refer back to what you wrote above. If a new fear occurs in this fear's place, repeat the process.

Depression, or Is It Appropriate Sadness?

Do not confuse depression with sadness. If you are crying a lot because you have lost someone through tragic and sudden death, you are sad, not depressed. If you find yourself immobilized, unable to concentrate, sleeping too much or too little, you are grieving, you are not depressed. Some other characteristics of this stage are:

- weakness and feeling drained
- loss of appetite
- extreme fatigue
- extreme irritability
- unresponsiveness
- inability to focus or concentrate
- feeling hopeless or powerless
- aches and pains
- lack of personal hygiene
- a feeling that the world is not a safe place

In her book *The Courage to Grieve,* Judy Tatelbaum writes, "So much of our energy is tied up inside that little energy is available for the action of functioning. We may be moody. At times we may feel pain and weep, and then at other times we may feel detached and without emotion. During this period we may be withdrawn and unable to relate to other people. Negativity, pessimism, emptiness, and a temporary sense of meaninglessness of life are all symptoms of depression. 'What's the use?' or 'Why bother?' are typical feelings. We may be acutely restless and then become immobile. The essential thing to remember is that the pain of grief is never constant and does not last forever. Throughout this middle phase of mourning, the myriad of feelings of grief come and go in waves, with lessening intensity as time goes on."

Again, if you feel stuck in this stage, you may need professional intervention. For most, however, this stage can be described as situational depression, meaning it should subside after a time.

Are you suffering from any of the above symptoms? If so, for how long? If these symptoms persist for more than six weeks or become troubling, seek professional help.

Loneliness

Whenever we feel the need to reach out yet no one is there to reciprocate, loneliness ensues. Sometimes our loneliness is valid—we don't have access to the specific help that we desire. At other times, loneliness is caused by our own choice not to reach out to others (unhealthy detachment).

Fortunately, loneliness is one of the emotions over which we have the most control. Thanks to the variety of support groups, the Internet, and our own personal circles, there is always someone we can reach out to, if we gather the energy to do so.

When do you experience your most intense loneliness?

_____

_____

_____

_____

Who do you know that you could seek support from in these lonely times? List them out below.

Name or Resource	Contact Information
Grief Steps Online	www.griefsteps.com

Calming Exercises

Stress, anxiety, sadness, depression—these emotions can leave us knotted inside. Practicing breathing exercises can help us to relax and to unwind our wound emotions. The following exercises will help calm you during trying times.

Place one hand on your abdomen. As you inhale, you want to feel the movement in your abdomen, not in your chest. Inhale for the count of ten, then exhale for the count of ten. Repeat this ten to fifteen times for deeper relaxation.

To relax your whole body, lie down in a quiet place. Breathe deeply, slowly inhaling and exhaling. Beginning with your left leg, clench your muscles as tightly as you can for the count of three. Then relax them. Do the same to the right leg, left arm, and right arm. Then move up your body, tightening your pelvis, then stomach, then chest, then shoulders, then neck, and lastly facial muscles. When you have completed this exercise, you should feel extremely calm and peaceful. Visualize an ocean beach or other calming scene to deepen the relaxed feelings.

If you like, record your visualization experience in the space below.

Multiple Grief

Some people have multiple situations they are dealing with on top of their grief. Perhaps an elderly parent is ill, you are sending a child off to college, you are going through menopause or a career change, or you are completing college or some other challenging life situation. These multiple situations can halt, delay, or complicate the primary grieving process. When we have many stressful experiences, much of our emotional energy is funneled into these stressors. We are left with little reserve. Yet in order to heal, we must find a way to cope with these stressors while still feeling and exploring our grief.

Although one experience may stand out in your mind, any other times of loss are likely to be important as well. Even things that might seem small or insignificant in the face of tragedy can complicate the grieving process when they accumulate. Soon we find ourselves stuck in a web of turmoil, unable to unravel our complicated feelings. Many events have mixed together and we can't pull on a single string to undo the knot—instead a tug on a single string just makes the knot tighter.

To work through multiple grief, it's important to recognize each of the components that you are grieving. Once you have identified those components, you can begin to focus on healing. Take your time in identifying these components—they may not come to the surface at first! If you find that you are still facing acute grief after a long period, you may want to come back to this exercise. Sometimes we suppress other losses that get caught up in the web. For example, a loss you are facing now might remind you of the absence of a parent during a difficult period in your life. Although this may not have been a death, it is a loss, and losses (not only deaths) are what lead to the experience of multiple grief.

What is the most recent experience you are grieving?

_____

_____

_____

_____

Are there any other experiences in the past five years that you grieved over?

_____

_____

_____

_____

_____

_____

_____

_____

For each of the experiences you listed, did you move through the different stages of grieving, or did you stop somewhere in the process without ever fully coming to terms with your grief? If you stopped grieving mid-process, where did you stop?

_____

_____

_____

_____

_____

_____

Are there any other times of loss your current experience resurrects in your mind?

_____

_____

_____

_____

When you have listed all of your grief you will know, because you will feel both a sadness and a relief inside. Until that point, you will feel a gnawing ache, as if you are trying to excavate a very embedded rock. You do not need to remember, recall, or record everything at once. Do not force it. Simply continue returning to this exercise, excavating a bit more each time.

Grief Sessions

Once you have listed out those things which you need to grieve in your life, you may find it helpful to schedule "Grief Sessions." Grief Sessions are set times where you honor your feelings. In our busy days, we tend to immerse ourselves in "things" so we don't experience our grief. But we can't get through what we do not feel.

Brook found it helpful to create a private space to grieve. Always the "strong" one in the family, she was unable to "break down" and grieve fully while in her house, or within her roles as mother, wife, and worker. She found that taking a day or a weekend to change her environment, even if it was to a cheap hotel, allowed her the space to let out and face her emotions.

Other people find success in spending an hour taking a walk and getting in touch with their grief. Some people can sit outside with a journal and express their feelings. Just as our grief is unique, so will our grief sessions be.

Write down some ideas for your own grief sessions—then schedule one on your calendar.

_____

_____

_____

_____

_____

_____

_____

_____

My first grief session will be on (list date/place):

_____

_____

_____

_____

Coping with Guilt

If you are suffering from the "if onlys" or the "I should haves," and you are left with a deep feeling of regret that you couldn't do more to help your loved one or prevent the death, try the following exercise:

Write at least a one-page letter to the individual who died. Tell them whatever you want, but remember to include the following:

- the facts of what happened
- how you feel about what happened
- how their death has affected your life

Now turn the page over and imagine the deceased responding to your letter. Asking questions of the deceased will make this exercise extremely valuable. So write down such questions as, "How do you feel about what happened?" and "Will you please forgive me for _____?" "Have I been punished enough for my part (real or imagined) in all this and is there anything else I can do to show you how sorry I am?" "How can I show you how much I have suffered?" Then close your eyes and answer each question as if they were speaking through you.

If you find this is a difficult exercise to do on your own, you may want to ask a therapist or trusted friend to sit quietly with you. **Caution:** If you are being "told" by your inner voice to hurt yourself in any way, seek professional help immediately.

Use the space below and on the following page to write a letter to your loved one.

_____

_____

Now write back to yourself, imagining how your loved one would respond.

Self-Check

As you work through your grief, it's important to monitor yourself and your stages. The following list can help you discern healthy grief from distorted grief. If you feel you may be suffering unhealthy grief, seek the help of a support group, clergyperson, or therapist.

❑ **Extreme Avoidant Behavior**—If you are avoiding friends and family for a prolonged period of time (over three weeks), you will want to talk to a professional. People need other people to work through grief.

❑ **Lack of Self-Care**—In order to have the energy and emotional capacity to work through grief, one must first take care of his or her basic needs. If you are having problems meeting basic needs, this is a warning sign to seek help.

❑ **Prolonged Denial**—If months have passed and you are still in denial, you will most likely need a support group to help you move through this stage.

❑ **Self-Destructive Thoughts**—These thoughts are not unusual during grief, but we can expect them to pass quickly. If they are persistent or obsessive, it is best to consult a professional for guidance in working through them.

❑ **Displaced Anger**—With few emotional outlets available to us, it is common for anger to be displaced. However, this can become problematic if your anger is hurting you in personal or professional areas, or hurting others—seek help immediately.

❑ **Prolonged Depression or Anxiety**—Like denial, prolonged and immobilizing depression or anxiety are signs to seek help.

❑ **Self-Medication**—If you are using substances in excess to self-medicate your pain (i.e. food, alcohol, or drugs), seek the help of an organization that specializes in such disorders or the help of a professional.

Chapter Four
Making Sense of the World Around You

SUGGESTED READING:

I Wasn't Ready to Say Goodbye
Chapter 5: The World is Upside Down

> The doorbell rang at around eight-thirty. I wasn't expecting anyone, so a strange feeling came over my heart. I peeked out the keyhole, and saw my brother, Denver, and sister-in-law, Allison, standing in the hallway. I let them in. There was a deep silence, and I knew from my brother's eyes what had happened. He didn't even have to speak. He took me in his arms, and my world changed forever. My eyes moved to a picture of my son as a child, his red hair cropped close to his head, and his big blue eyes looking out at me. My world was turning to darkness, and I would never live in it the same again."
> —*Singer Judy Collins on the death of her son, Clark.*

When we grapple with sudden loss, we are forced to reconsider some basic assumptions about ourselves. We may begin to feel vulnerable and a sense that life is tenuous. We may begin to question whether or not the world is meaningful and orderly. We may see ourselves as weak and needy for the first time. Those who haven't had to deal with the trauma of sudden death may also come to question these assumptions, but they are not *forced* to question the basic truth of these assumptions in the same way a survivor must.

We are all forced to confront our mortality. Most people deal with this issue in midlife. It is then that we begin to see signs of our own aging or we face the imminent death of our parents or grandparents. This is the natural order of things. However, as survivors of sudden death, we are forced to confront our mortality at the time of the trauma—regardless of our age. A heightened sense of the fundamental fragility of life quickly emerges—usually within minutes, hours, or days of the death.

Aphrodite Matsakis, PhD, says in her book, *Trust After Trauma*, "...although it can empower them to try to make the most out of life, it can also be frightening and overwhelming not only to themselves, but also to others who, quite understandably, prefer to avoid confronting the inevitability of their own deaths."

You may have thought, "It can't happen to me." But it did happen and you may no longer feel the world is a safe place. Feelings of vulnerability can bring on a sense of doom or an expectation that your own future may be foreshortened. You may also experience an intense fear that the trauma may repeat itself and another family member, lover, or friend will die.

Dr. Matsakis goes on to say, "The just world philosophy cannot explain what happened to you. You used to think that if you were careful, honest, and good, you could avoid disaster. But the trauma taught you that all your best efforts could not prevent the worst from happening. Perhaps you saw others who were also innocent die or who were unfairly injured. So, while you would like to believe that the world is orderly, and that good is rewarded and evil is punished, you had an experience that contradicts these beliefs."

When our foundation is swept from beneath us, we begin questioning the fundamentals of life. As crazy as it seems, this shattering of assumptions is a normal part of grief. *We must re-evaluate what we once held as true, move through the ruin, and create a new foundation based on what we have learned.*

What beliefs are you questioning? Remember, it's okay to question anything. Be true to yourself in your answer.

_____

_____

_____

_____

_____

_____

_____

_____

_____

_____

_____

_____

_____

_____

_____

_____

_____

_____

Loss of Purpose

Many grievers feel a loss of purpose. After all, we've known a life that is certain. We were certain that a person would be there, we never questioned. Suddenly, all we have left are questions—questions like: Why did this happen? If a person can die so suddenly—what is the purpose of trying to accomplish and trying to live? Brook battled this concept in the wake of Caleb's death.

I have always been an over-achiever. I scheduled and organized my life so I could climb mountain after mountain in search of reaching some higher place. When Caleb died, I wondered what the purpose of all the climbing was. I suddenly realized there was no guarantee I would live to be seventy—or even another week. So what was the purpose of all this sowing—if the chance to reap could be taken away?

Lost inside this question, I turned to a wonderful friend and my local pastor, Jeff. We often had lunch together and I always found comfort in his words. I stared at him across the table, and said simply—'What does anything matter?' He relayed a sentence, which was a riddle in itself. He simply said, 'Because nothing matters, everything matters.' I tried over lunch to comprehend the sentence as it twirled through my mind. Finally, I asked him to interpret further.

Jeff explained that looking long term or planning ahead cannot matter. Sure we need to be somewhat prepared for the future, but to become overly preoccupied is foolish since life can disappear so quickly. 'Everything you do at this very instant is what matters,' he explained. 'You should be living life, right now. Anyone who is living for tomorrow isn't really living' At the time, I had been juggling a few thoughts on where to go with my writing career and what project to pursue next. The thought of having a whole book in front of me seemed daunting and purposeless. I was scared to start something, scared perhaps that I would never finish it. Jeff asked me what mattered most at that very moment. "Getting by," was my reply. As our eyes met, I knew that was what mattered. I would write about getting by because that meant something to me, and if life went away tomorrow, I would be content in where I was today.

Since nothing of the future matters, everything in the here and now does. To learn to live in the present, to reap the gifts of the moment, is the best tribute we can give to anyone, much less ourselves.

How can you live "more in the moment" and less in the past and future?

_____

_____

_____

_____

_____

_____

When Faith is Shattered

If our spiritual faith has been shattered, perhaps all we can expect from the grieving process is some form of transcendence. Gail Sheehy describes this beautifully in her seminal work entitled, *Pathfinders*, where she writes, "Transcendence is a realm beyond all the negative emotions of mourning, beyond even the neutral point of acceptance. When it happens that a life accident creates a pathfinder, the person is able to transcend his former self as well. A positive self-fulfilling prophecy is made as one comes out of the dark hours. And around a new work, idea, purpose, faith, or a love inspired by the accident, one's goals are realigned. Transcendence is an act of creativity. One creates a partial replacement for what has been lost. The light at the end of mourning is glimpsed, and it is cause for new joy."

It's common to question God in these dark times. We may lose faith in God, a faith we thought would never change or waiver. In *The Grief Recovery Handbook,* John W. James and Russell Freidman write, "We have to be allowed to tell someone that we're angry at God and not be judged for it, or told that we're bad because of it. If not, this anger may persist forever and block spiritual growth. We've known people who never returned to their religion because they weren't allowed to express their true feelings. If this happens, the griever is cut off from one of the most powerful sources of support he or she might have."

For most of us, this loss of faith is temporary and if we ask our clergyperson or faith community, they should willingly help us with this struggle. It is common for grievers to yell, be angry, or scream at God. One should not feel guilty for such emotions. Like many other aspects of grief, this internal reckoning is part of the process. Even Pam's faith was tested during her experience with sudden loss . . .

> I remember walking up and down the halls of the hospital where George lay on life support, shaking my fist at Heaven, yelling at God. Someone who overheard suggested that I not be angry with God and that I control how I speak to Him. I replied, "My God can handle this anger. And I know if I get angry at God, God won't desert me."

The following anonymous poem can be comforting to recite when we are feeling lost and our faith is being tried.

Prayer of Faith

We trust that beyond absence
There is a presence.

That beyond the pain
there can be healing.

That beyond the brokenness
there can be wholeness.

That beyond the anger
there may be peace.

That beyond the hurting
there may be forgiveness.

That beyond the silence
there may be the Word.

That beyond the Word
there may be understanding.

That through understanding
there is love.

—author unknown

Are you angry at God? Write about your feelings honestly and openly in the space below.

_____

_____

_____

_____

_____

_____

How does this anger make you feel?

_____

_____

_____

_____

_____

_____

Are you in a faith community that can give you the support you need?

_____

_____

_____

_____

_____

_____

_____

_____

If not, is there another support community available to you?

_____

_____

_____

_____

_____

_____

_____

_____

If you find yourself in a faith community that cannot handle your anger, consider reevaluating your needs in time. Seek out a support group or community that can walk with you through this dark time. If your faith is important to you, do not shut yourself off from it for fear that no one will understand or accept you. After you have moved through your journey, you may want to consider going back to the faith community where you could not find initial support and begin a support group.

What Do I Believe?

As we stand at our own crossroad, we must look at our life and evaluate our faith. Is our faith a part of us, or is it simply something we have inherited and accepted blindly? Have we really believed prior to our loss—or have we just gone through the motions? What does faith mean to us? What do we seek to find? Once we identify our basic need and belief system, we can begin to move toward the communities and materials that will be the most helpful. Faith, by definition, should be something that encourages and supports us in our day-to-day living.

How did you come to your current faith?

_____

_____

_____

_____

_____

_____

_____

_____

_____

_____

_____

_____

_____

_____

_____

_____

Is your current faith supporting your needs?

_____

_____

_____

_____

_____

_____

_____

_____

_____

_____

_____

_____

_____

_____

_____

_____

_____

_____

_____

Writing a Prayer

Try writing a prayer sharing your feelings with God. Let Him know about your fears, your sadness, your doubts, your insecurities. The first step in healing any relationship is to relay how we feel. The same is true of your relationship with God. You may choose to keep an ongoing prayer journal.

Learning through Loss

Patricia lost her fourteen-year-old son, Doug, to a self-inflicted gunshot wound. She offers ten affirmations of life that she learned from her grieving process:

1. "I let my feelings flow; they are my life's blood; they will not kill me; they will heal me. (By the way, a punching bag is a good way to move from rage to tears.)
2. I follow my lead. I only need to know and then honor the next step.
3. I can trust the Universe to support me and it will in ways seen and unseen.
4. Help is there—I need only let it in at times, to ask others, and to trust that people want to help in these ways:
   Physically—mow my lawn, scrub my deck (where my son died)
   Metaphysically—pray for me, hold me in the light
   Psychologically—send me your memories of Doug, poems that mean something to you
5. I will confront my demons. Anxieties are not stoppers or signs to give up, they are just a new place to step slowly and to be creative.
6. Gratitude—every situation has a gift and a limit. I won't deny the limits and the pain and I will let myself see the gifts and the goodness as well.
7. Be there as a friend—the greatest gift I can give to someone is to accept him or her fully as they are.
8. Life is a journey, not a destination. I will live each day fully for its gifts of grief and gladness.
9. Grief comes in waves. Each carries me forward to the next step. An ocean never becomes stagnant water.
10. I will pray, meditate, and stay in touch with the spirit in whatever way works for me."

Patricia's final note: "Upon completion of this . . . a fresh wave of grief hit as spring and Easter arrived. I found myself needing to read what I had written over and over to remember the lessons I had so painfully learned. Which brings me to an old affirmation of mine . . . *I will tell a friend what I see as my truth so that someday when I forget, my friend can tell it back to me.* So dear reader, help me remember when times get tough."

Patricia chose to use the power of lessons learned in facing her grief. This practice is both healing and empowering. Try it for yourself. Purchase a small and beautiful bound book at a stationery store. In this book, record the lessons you learn moving through the grief process. It can be a great reminder of the steps you are taking and a wonderful way to become more aware of purpose and meaning. —Contributed by Patricia Ellen

On the following page, list lessons you have learned from your grief.

What I've Learned Along the Way

(see previous page for instructions)

What My Loved One Has Left Me

When someone dies suddenly, it is not unusual to have a sense that one was rejected or abandoned in some way. When you are feeling the searing pain and anger of abandonment, it is even more difficult to consider that your pain may be transformed into something meaningful or that the end of the relationship through death can be in any way beneficial to your growth. It can be, especially if you were dependent on the other person for good feelings about yourself. Now is the time to look within and to affirm yourself as a person of value. It is also the time to remember and replay the positive messages you heard from your significant other before they died. Everyone has heard at least one life-affirming, positive message from their deceased loved one worth repeating to oneself. List those messages in your journal or write them in letter form (i.e. Dear ___, these are the life affirming messages I bequeath to you. Love _____).

Allow these positive messages to lift and inspire you.

Record positive messages you received from your loved one in the space provided below. You may even want to photocopy this sheet and carry it with you for a time. Allow these positive messages to lift and inspire you.

_____

_____

_____

_____

_____

_____

_____

_____

_____

_____

Redefining Ourselves

When we lose someone, we often lose a piece of ourselves. The closer our relationship with the person, the more of our self we have to redefine. Much of our identity comes from our relationship to others. Take the woman who has called herself a wife and mother for thirty years and then loses her family in a plane crash. This woman whose identity was wife and mother is left without a husband or children. Defining ourselves by others can bring fullness to our lives, but when faced with loss it also means we must redefine the resulting emptiness.

One of the first things to remember when seeking redefinition is that you don't need to know all the answers now. No one should force you or "hold a clock to your head" asking you to redefine yourself overnight. This is a process. It involves soul-searching, courage, and rediscovery. It takes time. Realize that you don't have to let go of who you were—you just need to adapt for the future. In the case above, the mentioned woman will always know what it was like to be a wife and a mother. For the rest of her life, she will remember and relive her role in her thoughts and actions. Even though life turns itself upside down and our role may change suddenly, we can't deny the importance of our history.

Simply stated, the question becomes, "Now what?" After expecting life to take a certain course, it has chosen its own, far from your plans. Again, take it slow. Choose one thing that you know for certain. If you have always loved to paint, know that in the future you can still be a painter. Focus on what you do know about yourself. Look at the things you've always wanted to try and pick one to focus on. Take it one step at a time, and as you're ready, add another "piece" to yourself.

What are the things you know for certain?

_____

_____

_____

_____

_____

_____

_____

For some, this rebuilding takes months, for others it can take a lifetime, but piece by piece you can rebuild. When you are ready to begin the rebuilding process, try the exercises on the following pages.

Thank You Exercise

As you continue to grow and heal, you will eventually discover at least something (no matter how seemingly insignificant) for which you can express gratitude. If the expression is not available to you now, it is probably a temporary condition.

After you have honored your anger, and when you are ready, you might want to try this Thank You Exercise. Compared to all other acts, personal and spiritual growth is greatest through the expression of gratitude. No matter how difficult at first, expressing appreciation for the life that is gone can help make some meaning in the face of tragedy. Acknowledging, in writing, what was empowering and uplifting about your relationship to the deceased will help you keep sacred what you had together—to retain what was valuable and to let go of the false belief that they are incapable of inspiring you (now that they are dead.)

Why pick up a pen and write a note—why not just think about it? The act of writing, choosing the type of pen and paper, the color of the ink, moving the pen across the paper, seeing the words—all make what you are saying more real—more concrete. You will notice your energy shift—from confusion about what to write, anger at having to sort through your life for the first time (or the thousandth time), tears as you recognize what you have lost, and ultimately a sense of relief at having given yourself the chance to express the unsaid.

Date and save your notes in a special place or put them in your journal. You may want to destroy the note. Remember, this is about expressing feelings that need to be expressed. Rereading it again, however, after several months or years, is sometimes useful, so you may want to save it for future reference. It is also useful to write another note after some time has passed. Each time you write, you will gain new insights. If you have young children, you may even want to read it to them when they are older.

You will find an example on the following page.

59

Dear Jim, Thanks for the holding. You were good at holding when I needed to be held—when I was having trouble learning to trust—you helped me to know that I was capable of loving.

You held me when I was sad. I had so much sadness then. Thank you for the many times you were able to say, "Everything will be all right." Thank you for coming into this lifetime. This time I received the lesson I was so long denying that I needed to learn. What did I learn? I learned that it is unwise to marry someone to give you what you didn't get from your parents as a child. It is important to nurture and love yourself.

Thank you for being a good father to our son—you were the kind of father I would have wanted for myself. Thank you for the ten years of our marriage—for ten years I felt loved. Thanks for being with me at the birth of our son and for supporting us so I could stay home with him when he was a baby—yes, MOST OF ALL, thank you for our son for without you, he would not have been born. Love, Joan

Although she sobbed on and off for the better part of an hour after writing this, Joan admitted to experiencing a sense of relief and to feeling better about herself than she had in some time. She affirmed why she had chosen the man she did and felt great comfort in expressing her appreciation for her husband in her letter to him.

Use the space on the following page to write your own Thank You Letter when you are ready.

Thank You Letter

Finding a Beginning, Middle, and End

Questions abound when we lose someone tragically. Unlike those who lose someone after a lengthy illness, we have little or no time to question doctors, understand a diagnosis, struggle with our faith, or say our goodbyes.

During our upbringing we learn to understand life in terms of cycles. We understand the cycle of age. We know the cycle of schooling. We know the cycle of work. We know the cycles of diet and exercise. Almost everything can be understood as a cycle with a beginning, middle, and end. Our minds will immediately try to do the same with our tragic loss experience. Our mind will look for the beginning (What happened?), the middle (How did he/she feel, respond, progress?), the end (Was he in pain? Did he have any last thoughts or words?) Yet unless we were present, we are left with question after question. In order to get to a place where we can think about the experience in its entirety, we must know as much of the cycle as possible.

This is why it is so natural to talk with others about our loved one's last moments. Over and over again, grievers tell their stories, attempting to make sense of them, attempting to understand the cycle. Often, there are ways to get more information. Police, witnesses, and doctors can all offer clues to what happened. When we have enough clues we can piece together a story that will allow our questioning to lessen. As our questions lessen, we create more room to heal.

Dr. Ann Kaiser Stearns, author of *Coming Back: Rebuilding Lives After Crisis and Loss,* offers the following suggestion: "Make a conscious effort to identify what is not making sense to you about your loss or crisis. You might ask yourself: What is it about the situation and/or about his or her death that is most puzzling or troubling to me? What part of grief is troubling me? What other things are troubling me?"

Before seeking your own beginning, middle and end, this can be a useful exercise. Confront your questions. Explore your feelings and record these thoughts. Use this as a guideline to gather the information you will need.

Brook found that she and her mother had many questions.

> "For starters, my mother and I had never heard of the term anaphylactic shock—we couldn't even pronounce it. Our initial disbelief was so strong, not a single question was asked at the hospital. But as the days went by, the questions came one after the other. *Caleb had been stung a month before—was this a cumulative effect of venom? A long time ago he had chest pains that went undiagnosed—could his death be connected to that? Had any blood been drawn and a firm allergic reaction determined? If his death certificate said 12:54 and his friends said he was unconscious at 11:15—what happened between then and 12:54?*

I did as much research as I could and then I called the doctor. I immediately put him at rest by letting him know that I trusted he had done everything in his capacity, and I did not, in any way, question his ability. I let the doctor know that my questions were more about figuring out the order of events. We talked for close to an hour.

After combining his comments with my research, I was able to confidently assume that Caleb did die from a fatal reaction to a bee sting. He was dead before the ambulance arrived, or minutes after, and unconscious long before that. He was not pronounced dead until 12:54 because the doctors were praying for a miracle. Being so young and healthy, they worked extensively on him in the E.R. trying anything they could to revive him.

I learned bee allergies are not hereditary. However, I also discovered those who know they are allergic can carry an Epinephrine shot. Epinephrine can relieve the reaction or buy the needed time to get treatment.

With this knowledge and for my own peace of mind, I went to a specialist in the allergy field. I asked the allergist to test both my three-year-old daughter and myself. He took our blood and sent it to the Mayo clinic for analysis. The tests came back negative. Yet, since this allergy can develop at any time, he gave us both adrenaline kits so that we would feel more at ease. While only ten people a year die from fatal reactions to insects, it was important for me to have that comfort."

Talking to others will help you get the information you need to find your own beginning, middle, and end. This information-gathering can be a major catalyst in moving past the grief of "what happened?" to the process of rebuilding. It allows the mind to cycle through the event in its entirety, instead of stopping to question and get lost in the who, what, when, where, why, and how.

What do you know for certain about the death of your loved one?

_____

_____

_____

_____

_____

What questions do you have?

_____

_____

_____

_____

_____

Can you research the answers to those questions or contact someone to help you find the answers?

_____

_____

_____

_____

_____

_____

_____

When will you contact that person or do the research?

_____

_____

What information did you learn from your research?

_____

_____

_____

_____

_____

_____

_____

_____

Take a page or two to write the beginning, middle, and end of *your* story.

_____

_____

_____

_____

_____

_____

_____

_____

_____

_____

_____

_____

_____

_____

Chapter Five
Grief Blocks

SUGGESTED READING:

I Wasn't Ready to Say Goodbye
Chapter 4: Myths and Misunderstandings of the Grieving Process

> "It comes to all. We know not when,
> or how, or why. It's always been
> a mystery, a frightening thing,
> enshrouded in the silencing.
> When suddenly a loved one dies
> we seem to sort of paralyze,
> to just stop still within our track.
> And oh, how much we want them back."
> *—excerpted from "When a Loved One Dies,"*
> *by Dolores Dahl, Suddenly Alone*

Grieving is like a foreign land to most of us; a land where we find ourselves speaking and hearing an inner language we cannot comprehend. Because it can help to have a guide in our foreign land, this chapter will describe ways we commonly avoid grief and why we do so.

I Don't Want to Talk About It

You've got to talk about it, and talk about it, and talk about it some more. Find someone who will listen and talk until you can't talk anymore . . . at least for the moment. Then when you need to talk again, start all over with your story. Talking about it is an extremely important task. If you try to skip it, you will be blocked indefinitely. It is a task that will help you come to terms with the death and move you past the denial stage.

If you don't want to talk about it, try writing about it by answering the questions on the following pages. Answering these questions will not be a pleasant task and is not necessary if you are healthily talking through your experience with others. These questions are simply for those who are using avoidant behavior. Before we can heal, we must acknowledge. These questions serve as a step toward acknowledgement for those who are not talking with others.

Acknowledgement (see previous page to see if this is a page you need to complete)

The person I loved and lost was . . . _____

Describe briefly the circumstances of the death. _____

_____

_____

_____

_____

_____

When I talk about my loss, I feel . . . _____

_____

_____

_____

_____

_____

I am scared that . . . _____

_____

_____

_____

Write down the name of a trusted friend, clergyperson, or professional with whom you could attempt to discuss your loss. _____

Help, I'm Stuck on Instant Replay

One of the horrors of instant replay is the persistent questioning of the choices we made. For example: Could I have called the ambulance sooner? If I'd known CPR would it have made a difference? Were there warning signs of the condition that I missed? Could I have done anything at all to prevent it? This kind of constant replay over an extended period blocks acceptance and closure.

Instant replay is the mind's way of coming to terms with the unfathomable. Some instant replay is necessary, but too much can keep us stuck. If your own instant replay is becoming an obsession, make an effort to do what therapists call "thought stopping." This is a technique whereby you consciously stop the thought, and deliberately change the subject. This is not a complicated task and is easier to do than you might think.

If the deceased's death was particularly troubling, you may be replaying it over and over in your mind. If you have a horrible image of your loved one's last minutes or hours that runs over and over like a bad movie, first acknowledge the horror, and then shift to an image of when you first met. Replace one image with the other.

Paul G. Stoltz, PhD, writes in his book entitled, *Adversity Quotient: Turning Obstacles into Opportunities:* "Arm yourself with STOPPERS. Whenever a crisis strikes, anxiety is a frequent—and useless—response. It also spreads like an emotional wildfire making it impossible to apply rational steps to better cope with the problem. Soon you start to 'catastrophize' and feel helpless and hopeless. You squander energy and time worrying. To avoid imagining the worst will happen, use what I call 'stoppers' to regain control."

He continues, "When you feel overwhelmed, slap your knee or any hard surface. Shout, "Stop!" The sting will shock you into a more rational state. Some people leave a rubber band around their wrist. When they feel anxiety, they stretch it six inches, and let it go.

Focus intently on an irrelevant object, such as a pen, the pattern of the wallpaper, or a piece of furniture. If your mind is removed from the crisis, even for a moment, you can return with the calm you need to take effective action.

Take an activity break. Just fifteen or twenty minutes of brisk walking or other exercise will clear your mind, raise your energy, and flood your brain with endorphins—chemicals that put you in a more optimistic mood.

Put yourself in a setting where you're dwarfed by your surroundings. Catastrophizing makes problems larger than life. A shift in perspective will cut them down to size. Drive to the beach and look out over the ocean . . . stand at the base of a large tree . . . gaze up at the clouds . . . or listen to a great piece of music and let the grandeur wash over you."

What "STOPPER" can you try when you hit an instant replay? (See Chapter 4).

_____

_____

_____

_____

Self-Judgment

Here is a sample of some internal, self-judging statements: "I'm not grieving right, I should be doing it differently. Perhaps I went back to work too soon. If I really loved him (or her), I'd be more devastated!"

This kind of self-judgment can block grief and is self-defeating at best. Perhaps you are looking at the way others grieve and are comparing yourself to them. Just as no two people are alike on this planet, no two people will "do grief" in exactly the same way. Some people will function at a very high level and some will not function at all. Some people will become introspective, others will cry, rant, scream, and rage at the drop of a hat. These differences are largely influenced by the stage of grief you are in and your personality type. Cultural differences are also at play here, and men have a tendency to grieve differently than women. Another important variable, is the number of losses you have experienced in your life. Multiple losses compound and will influence how you handle your grief. (see page 38 for more on Multiple Grief.) We've said it many times: we all grieve in our own unique way. Stop the judgment and remove this block to healthy grief.

What unrealistic expectations do you have about the grieving process?

_____

_____

_____

Write a short note forgiving yourself for your hurtful self-talk; or write down the hurtful things you say on a separate piece of paper. Then rip it up and throw it out as a symbol of your release from self-judgement.

_____

_____

_____

_____

_____

_____

_____

_____

_____

_____

_____

_____

_____

I Feel So Guilty

In this case, you may be blocked by self-blame and you may be suffering from what is called, "survivor guilt." In *Survivor Guilt* author Aphrodite Matsakis, Ph.D, writes that; "Survivor guilt involves asking the existential question of why you suffer less than someone else, or why you lived while others died."

Of all the blocks mentioned in this chapter, guilt may be the strongest of all. Struggling with the question, "Why them, not me?" can create so much anxiety, pain and self-doubt that you stay stuck in your grief, much longer and more intensely than needed. You may feel that guilt is the way to "pay penance" for surviving, or that intense guilt is a way to honor your lost loved one. However, they want more for us, much more. Process your guilt with a trusted friend, therapist, or clergyperson. The best way to honor the deceased is to move through your guilt, put down the stick you use to beat yourself with, and move on. (See the Guilt worksheet and exercise on page 113 for further assistance.)

You may also want to try and take a fresh perspective. What do you think your loved . . . one would tell you about the guilt you are feeling? Write your thoughts below.

_____

_____

_____

_____

_____

_____

_____

_____

_____

_____

Grief Myths

Grieving is like a foreign land to most of us, a land where we find ourselves speaking and hearing an inner language we cannot comprehend. Because it can help to have a guide in a foreign land, this chapter will describe the common myths and misunderstandings to help you navigate the territory within.

It is the rare school or family environment that teaches what to expect either emotionally or pragmatically when life collapses in tragedy, especially with the advent of sudden and unexpected death. A sudden loss can put one into a whirlwind of emotions and visceral responses, twisting and turning us until we are set down in a place that feels as foreign as another planet. Like a tornado, there is no time for preparations. We have little or no warning.

In Chapter 4 of *I Wasn't Ready to Say Goodbye*, we explore the twenty-seven most common myths and misunderstandings about grief listed below. Read through Chapter 4 and mark any of the myths you have been influenced by below. When you are finished, rewrite a new understanding to take the place of the outdated myth or misunderstanding.

> Myth #1 Death is death, sudden or long term, and we all grieve the same way.
>
> Myth #2 By keeping busy I can lessen or eliminate my grief.
>
> Myth #3 I am going crazy or "losing it."
>
> Myth #4 I will need to make sure I don't grieve for too long—one year should be enough.
>
> Myth #5 If I express my anger at God or the circumstances of the death, I am a bad person and will "pay" for it.
>
> Myth #6 I must wear black for a designated time period or I will dishonor the person who died.
>
> Myth #7 I won't have to grieve as much and I will feel better if I use alcohol or medication to alleviate my sadness.
>
> Myth #8 My friends tell me it is time to let go. Since others have acclimated to life again, I should too.
>
> Myth #9 If I talk about the loss of my loved one I'll feel worse.
>
> Myth #10 I should be strong enough to "tough it out" by myself.
>
> Myth #11 I've done something wrong because some of my family and friends are turning away from me.
>
> Myth #12 I should be relieved that they didn't suffer a long and lingering illness.
>
> Myth #13 Someday I'll have another (spouse, child, parent, lover . . .) and that person will erase the pain and replace what I have lost.
>
> Myth #14 Once I am done with one stage of grief, I move on to the next.

Myth #15 If I relive the good times, I'll stay stuck in the pain.

Myth #16 Children really don't understand death and probably don't need to be included in the funeral plans or memorial services.

Myth #17 To properly honor the deceased, I must have the standard wake and burial.

Myth #18 I am scared that if I grieve, I'll "get over my loss." I don't want to forget him!

Myth #19 I'm stuck on instant replay. I can't get this out of my thoughts—something is wrong with me.

Myth #20 This kind of thing doesn't happen in my family

Myth #21 Medication can help me avoid the whole grieving process.

Myth #22 There must be something wrong with me. I'm not crying

Myth #23 I'm not grieving right—I should be doing something differently.

Myth #24 I should feel guilty.

Myth #26 I'll never be happy again.

Myth #27 In order to process my grief effectively I need to advance through the Five Stages of Grief.

Myth #28 The final stage of grieving is acceptance.

Write down a myth or misunderstanding that has impacted your journey through grief.

_____

_____

What is a new belief that you can put in the place of this outdated myth or misunderstanding?

_____

_____

_____

_____

_____

_____

Write down a myth or misunderstanding that has impacted your journey through grief.

_____

_____

What is a new belief that you can put in the place of this outdated myth or misunderstanding?

_____

_____

_____

Write down a myth or misunderstanding that has impacted your journey through grief.

_____

_____

_____

What is a new belief that you can put in the place of this outdated myth or misunderstanding?

_____

_____

_____

Write down a myth or misunderstanding that has impacted your journey through grief.

_____

_____

_____

What is a new belief that you can put in the place of this outdated myth or misunderstanding?

_____

_____

_____

_____

Write down a myth or misunderstanding that has impacted your journey through grief.

_____

_____

What is a new belief that you can put in the place of this outdated myth or misunderstanding?

_____

_____

_____

_____

Hurtful Self-Talk

Be aware of the following hurtful self-talk that can block the grieving process—keeping you stuck. The following statements are examples of commonly held misconceptions that may run through our minds.

- My loved one is with God for a reason, so I shouldn't feel bad.
- Grief is a mental illness.
- It is wrong to feel anger at the deceased and it shouldn't be expressed.
- If I acknowledge the loss, I'm afraid I will die too.
- I should have died first.

- If I allow my grief to surface, I'll go crazy.
- If I grieve, people will think I'm weak.
- If I appear sad too often, it will bring my family down.
- If I cry in church, my fellow congregants will think I've lost faith.
- If my children see me grieving, it will make them feel worse.
- The deceased wouldn't want me to grieve.
- I should grin and bear it and put it behind me.
- If I stop grieving people will expect me to be happy again.

When you find yourself running on the treadmill of hurtful self-talk, it is important to come up with a positive statement for balance. Write down your destructive or hurtful thought and then write down a more positive, realistic thought. For example, "The deceased wouldn't want me to grieve," is an unhelpful statement. You could write, "The deceased would understand and respect the full spectrum of my emotions." Whenever a negative thought enters your mind, replace it with a positive, more realistic statement.

Try "reprogramming" your hurtful self-talk below on the following page. Continue to add statements along with their positive counterparts as they occur to you throughout your journey.

Reprogramming Self-Talk

Hurtful Statement:

_____

_____

Positive Statement:

_____

_____

Hurtful Statement:

_____

Positive Statement:

_____

_____

Hurtful Statement:

_____

_____

Positive Statement:

_____

_____

Chapter Six
Helping Children Cope with Grief

 **SUGGESTED READING:**
I Wasn't Ready to Say Goodbye
Chapter 9: Helping Children Grieve

> "In one of the stars
> I shall be living
> In one of them
> I shall be laughing
> And so it will be
> As if all the stars
> Were laughing
> When you look
> At the sky at night"
> —*Antoine de Saint-Exupéry,*
> **The Little Prince**

As children grow, they will need to re-experience the loss at each stage of development. For example, at age five, a child's understanding of death has moved from fantasy-based to reality-based. As they learn and understand more, they may need to review and re-experience the loss. When children realize the finality of death, they need to re-interpret what the death means to them. It's important to know this so that you don't feel you are "taking two steps backward," if your child becomes preoccupied with the loss at different stages of his or her development.

One of the biggest challenges for children is the loss of their assumption that childhood is a safe place. Until this moment, young children believe they are immortal and invulnerable and that nothing could hurt their friends, parents, or siblings. This deep trust is destroyed when they experience tragic loss at a young age.

A child's actions may change. It is not uncommon for a child to emotionally and physically regress during the grief process. The child may lash out, throw temper tantrums, do poorly in school, become shy or introverted, perform badly at once-perfected skills, have nightmares, and the like.

Patience and love are the keys to helping your child move past regression. This patience and love is only possible if you are doing your own grief work and renewing yourself emotionally.

Below you will find some common reactions children face while grieving:

Private Grieving

Children usually aren't as familiar and in tune with their emotions as adults. For this reason, many grieve privately. They may cry in their rooms or in the shower.

Unhealthy Anger

Children may choose unhealthy venues for releasing their anger. They may destroy things or engage in self-destructive behavior. It's important to remember that children do not have as many healthy outlets open to them as adults do. For this reason, it is imperative that we offer healthy outlets to teenagers.

Review the pages on Anger (30–32). Below, list several ways you, or another trusted adult, can help your child with this emotion.

_____

_____

_____

_____

Sexual Activity in Older Children

With the loneliness that accompanies grief, teenagers may be left feeling lonely and scared. They may feel family members don't have the energy or ability to comfort them, since they are facing their own grief. For these reasons, it is not uncommon for teenagers to become sexually active in an attempt to ease the loneliness. If you are concerned that your child may become sexually active try talking to your child, or ask another trusted adult to broach the subject.

Guilty Feelings

From an early age, children long to please their parents, family members, and those close to them. Often they interpret an argument as their failure to please. Furthermore, they may feel responsible for the death because they didn't behave well, caused too many arguments, were a source of stress, or didn't meet parents' expectations. While parents find this reasoning inconceivable, it is common in a teenager's mind. It is important to reiterate over and over again that the teenager was in no way responsible for the death. Older children may find the guilt exercise on page 113 helpful.

Physical Outbursts

Since children are less mature emotionally, they are much more likely to act out their emotions physically. This can take the form of tantrums, fighting, screaming, tattooing, body piercing, or other physical expression. Watch for these physical signs. When you see one, realize it is probably caused by emotional repression. Take this as a red flag to find a support network or professional intervention for your child.

The Need to Be Away From Home (in Older Children)

When the deceased is a sibling, adolescents and teens may want to be away from the house. There are a couple of reasons for this. First, parents may be so absorbed in their own grief that children do not want to intensify their own emotions and grief by being around their parents. They may feel an obligation to comfort parents, yet they may not have the emotional energy to do so. Second, the house carries many memories of the relationship with their sibling and they may not be ready to face these memories. While it's important to maintain communication with the child and discuss their feelings, also offer the child his/her needed space, provided it's safe space.

Suicidal Thoughts

If the child was especially close to the person they have lost, they may see suicide as a way to rejoin their loved one. Also, when children are not dealing with their emotions in a healthy way, they can quickly become overwhelmed. Suicide becomes an escape route from these turbulent emotions. When a child mentions or details any part of a suicidal plan, recognize this as an immediate sign to seek professional help.

Love and Support

During your child's grief, it is important to assure him or her of your love. Take a moment to write a letter to your child explaining your love for him, what you are proud of, how you sympathize and let your child know that you are there for him. Although he or she may not comment on your letter, behind closed doors it will be appreciated and re-read.

In the space provided below, outline the points you would like to cover in your letter.

General Guidelines for Helping Children

Below you will find some guidelines to review, as you work to understand your children's experience and help them through their grief.

- To help the child begin to mourn, a surviving parent needs to continue the daily routine as much as possible.
- Work on listening. Communicating with a different generation can be difficult. Do your best to listen and be present without telling the child what to do. If you have a hard time listening objectively, find someone who can.
- Continually express your unconditional love and acceptance.
- The child's environment should stay the same—this is not the time for a new school, a new house, or even a new babysitter.
- When you sense the child's readiness to grieve, it is okay to pray together, cry together, and reminisce together.
- Allow the child to talk, and talk, and talk about the death with you. Help him or her understand that the intensity of grief will lessen over time. Not talking about death (which indicates that the subject is off-limits) does not help children learn to cope with loss.
- When discussing death with children, explanations should be simple and direct. Each child should be told the truth using as much detail as he or she is able to understand. The child's questions should be answered honestly and directly.
- Children need to be reassured about their own security (they often worry that they will also die, or that their surviving parent will go away). Children's questions should be answered, making sure that the child understands the answers.
- A discussion about death should include the proper words, such as car accident, died, and death. Substitute words or phrases (for example, "he passed away," "he is sleeping," or "we lost him") should never be used because they can confuse children and lead to misunderstandings.
- When a death occurs, children can and should be included in the planning and participation of memorial ceremonies. These events help children (and adults) remember loved ones. Children should not be forced to be involved in these ceremonies, but they should be encouraged to take part in those portions of the events with which they feel most comfortable. If the child wants to attend the funeral, wake, or memorial service, he or she should be given in advance a full explanation of what to expect.

Remember that no matter how old the child, they have experienced the worst possible tragedy. They will feel terrible. They should not be encouraged to forget or deny. They must learn, with your help and guidance, that they can overcome emotional catastrophes. Allowing the child to feel the full power of the sudden loss will help increase coping ability for the rest of the child's life.

Take a moment to think about your child. What information and support do they need from you? How can you help? What questions could you ask? What information could you share? Write down your thoughts below.

One of the hardest challenges of parenting is seeing a child in pain. We are used to being able to "fix everything" and "make it okay." Grief cannot be fixed, it can only be worked through. Focus on how you can be a strength and anchor for your child.

_____

_____

_____

Tips for Older Children

- ❑ Ask to see a picture of the person the child has lost. Ask questions about the person. Ask them to share their favorite stories and memories.

- ❑ Be inquisitive about the death. Ask the child what happened. Ask how the child feels about what happened. Often, as a teenager tells their story, we can listen carefully for clues of what they are confused about or feeling guilty for.

- ❑ Talk to your teenager about grief and the common emotions he/she is likely to feel. If it is the child's first time with these intense feelings, they can be extremely frightening. Choose a book or two from the recommended resources list to help the teenager familiarize himself with the emotions of grief.

- ❑ Encourage the teenager to make a collage. Help to gather magazines and pictures. Cut out words, pictures, and notes that carry special memories. Place the finished collage in a place where the teen can see it often.

- ❑ Consider framing a picture of their loved one and hanging it in their room.

❑ Help the teenager identify his needs and relate them to others. A teenager may feel unsupported, but it's hard for others to support him when they don't understand these needs. Identifying what would help most is a way to alleviate the unneeded pain of isolation.

❑ Encourage your teen to start a support group with other grieving friends. Offer your home as a safe place to hold the meetings. Do whatever you can to help. Perhaps you could carpool and pick up other kids, provide appetizers, or beverages, photocopy handouts, etc.

Take a moment to think about your child. What information and support do they need from you? How can you help? What questions could you ask? What information could you share? Write down your thoughts below.

Chapter Seven
Special Occasions and Challenges

 SUGGESTED READING:
I Wasn't Ready to Say Goodbye
Chapter 7: Difficult Days: Holidays, Anniversaries, and More

> Traditions are like rules; however well intentioned when it comes down to
> it, they were made to be broken. As children we lived for the opportunity to
> break rules and traditions, to strike out on a different path. Why not
> experience that joy? Change the meal, change the location, make new
> traditions; your life has changed tremendously
> and so should your traditions."
> —*Scott Miller,* **Tips for Those Grieving During the Holiday Season**

Holidays, birthdays, and other special days associated with the deceased present a special challenge. The loss becomes painfully evident and the feelings associated with the occasion become dulled and gray. Try not to be alarmed by occasional setbacks. This chapter will give you some ideas about what to expect. Knowing what to expect will allow you to create some options for yourself when these situations arise.

Birthdays

The deceased person's birthday is a time for remembering. You may feel your loss anew for many years each time their birthday comes.

Your own birthday may seem different. You may wonder why you are still alive and they are not, and it will be difficult to celebrate your own life for a while. For those who have lost an older sibling, the year when you pass your sibling's age at their time of death can be incredibly stressful. It is an odd feeling to outlive your older sibling.

Many people find a sanctuary by creating a ritual with which to celebrate the deceased's birthday. Perhaps you can surround yourself with other people who were close to the loved one. Perhaps you can go take a walk in nature and just think and cry and rant and talk out loud. In the Exercises chapter you will find some rituals that may be useful.

Anniversaries

Some people find that they may do well for an entire year, only to find themselves virtually incapacitated by grief during the days surrounding the anniversary of the death. You wake up one morning with a heavy feeling, not knowing exactly why you feel so burdened. Then it hits you—the anniversary of one or another dates you shared with the deceased in the past.

On the anniversary of the day of death, many grievers report a short-term depression. It's not uncommon to experience discomfort, sadness, and depression for a couple weeks before and after the date of death each year. You may find some alternative solutions like herbs, vitamins, and therapy to help you through this trying time. The strength of a support network can also be beneficial. Many people do "fine" throughout the year, only to be knocked off their feet as these significant dates occur.

Some religious traditions have a requirement based on the one year anniversary of the death. In Judaism for instance, Judaic law has a prescribed ritual for "death days"—the anniversary of the death. You are expected to need to discharge extra emotions during those days. The headstone is unveiled a year later. Every following year, a special candle is lit in the home. Even if your religious tradition does not dictate it, you will feel some deep or extreme emotion on the anniversary of the death. Try to look at the anniversary of the death as another opportunity to grieve—to feel some of what has been unexpressed up until now.

Other anniversaries where you can expect to feel "extra emotions" include:

the last day you saw your loved one alive
the day you first met
the day you were married or engaged
the day the "plug" was pulled
the day you found out they were dead
the anniversary of a trip you took together

There may be additional anniversaries depending on your relationship to the deceased. If you expect these anniversaries to be challenging emotional times, you will be less surprised. If you know they are coming and when, you will be better able to cope. Mark your calendar and make special plans. If you can, make special arrangements for yourself (i.e. take the day off from work, get a babysitter for the kids, find time and space to be alone, visit the grave, etc.) You may want to consider a ritual for the day of death. The exercises section of this book contains several ideas. You may also want to consider one of the rituals that follow.

Rituals

Rituals are an important part of life. Through rituals we are able to observe, remember and structure our beliefs and feelings. In her book, *Surviving Grief*, Dr. Catherine M. Sanders writes, "In the past, rites of passage for every shift point in life were marked by rituals, which commanded a respected place in our culture. Large extended families came together to honor the person being celebrated. During chaotic times of change and transition, these rituals provided important direction and spiritual strength."

Funeral services are an example of a ritual. They give us guidance and direction that allows us to come together and celebrate life with those who share our loss.

Creating your own ritual may seem like a difficult task, but it doesn't have to be. To begin, ask yourself what you are trying to remember or celebrate. For many, a ritual on the anniversary date of the death is valuable. Others find they'd like to create a ritual for the birthday of the deceased. If the deceased was a spouse, the wedding anniversary may be a good time for a ritual. There are no limits on rituals. You can have one each season of the year, or one annually or every other year. Think about the purpose of your ritual as you decide on frequency. For most who are grieving, the ritual period becomes a time of breaking away from the day-to-day demands so we can experience our grief fully and focus on the memories we hold of our loved one.

Next, decide if you want the ritual to be just for yourself or if you want to share it with others. You may find that having a group of friends engage in the ritual is helpful. Others like this time to explore their emotions by themselves.

Where you should conduct your ritual is the next question to answer. There may be a special place that you associate with the deceased. You may want to stay close to home or you may wish to travel overseas. Again, keep your purpose in mind as you choose your location.

Here are a few rituals that those who we've known have conducted and found comforting. Feel free to conform these to rituals that suit your needs or to use them as a springboard for other ideas.

Karen was living in France when her mother died suddenly at the age of fifty, leaving her father alone in the United States. Each year, Karen returns home for a week over the anniversary of her mother's death. She and her father use this time to recall their memories and visit the grave site.

Jessica, Monica, Laura, and Allie were close college friends, all living together. When Laura was killed suddenly in a car accident, the other three young women were torn apart. Each year, on the anniversary of the death, the three women get together and take a cruise. They recall their fun college days together. It has been five years since these women graduated, and they still continue with this ritual.

David wanted to be alone on his deceased son's birthday. He rented a small cabin in the mountains and took nothing with him but spare clothes. He walked in the mountains, absorbed the beautiful scenery, and "talked" to his son.

Cassandra, a single mother, was lost after the sudden death of her daughter. On the anniversary of her death, she asked her ex-husband to watch their other children. She took the weekend to write, cry, watch movies, and look through old photos.

Take some quiet time to sit and think about what might help you to heal. Then commit to a ritual. Mark off the dates on your calendar.

Ideas for Remembrance from the American Association of Retired Persons

From photo collages at a memorial service to planting a tree, there are many ways we can say, "I remember and loved this person." As you consider how you might want to remember a loved one, here are some ideas to start with. Consider:

- Lighting a candle in her memory
- Creating a memory book of photos of your loved one
- Donating a gift of money or time to those less fortunate
- Wearing a photo pin of your loved one
- Starting a memorial scholarship fund in his name
- Writing a poem or story about him
- Visiting a place you both liked to visit
- Hanging a special ornament on the tree in her memory
- Playing her favorite music
- Making a quilt from his favorite clothes
- Sharing memories of her with friends and family
- Providing memorial flowers for her at your church or synagogue
- Creating a memory box of items that were special
- Honoring his favorite tradition
- Creating a new tradition in your memory
- Hanging a stocking filled with loving memories of him

- Gathering your family and friends together in celebration of him
- Reading aloud your favorite story

The AARP provides a discussion area to share ideas and suggestions for the honoring of a loved one at community.aarp.org/rp-griefnloss/start.

Which of the above ideas sounds comforting to you? Make a few notes of what would be comforting in your time of need. Take some quiet time to sit and think about what might help you to heal. Feel free to conform these rituals to suit your own needs, or to use them as springboards for your own ideas. Then commit to a ritual. Mark off the dates on your calendar.

_____

_____

_____

_____

_____

_____

_____

_____

_____

_____

_____

_____

_____

_____

Holidays

With the loss of a member of your immediate family, holidays and special occasions will be difficult. Holidays are often filled with traditions and memories of closeness. As we face these days without our loved one, the empty space they leave behind looms large in our hearts. By creating new traditions and understanding the common difficulties faced during the holidays, they can be easier to cope with.

The American Association of Retired Persons offers the following tips in their article, "Frequently Asked Questions by the Widowed." (Italics ours.)

Plan ahead. It helps to ease the strain.

Where will you be for the holidays?

_____

_____

Set priorities. This can make it easier to phase out elements less pleasing to you.

Are there any holiday activities you do not want to participate in?

_____

_____

Make new traditions. This new phase in your life deserves some new traditions.

What is a new tradition you could try? See the following page for additional suggestions and ideas.

_____

_____

Include [the deceased's] name in conversation. It helps others talk about him/her.

What story could you share with others this holiday season?

_____

_____

Express your feelings. Most people understand and accept your need to cry.

Find someone you can help. Giving assistance to others is very satisfying.

Who could you help this holiday season?

_____

_____

Buy yourself something special. You've suffered a great loss. Be good to yourself.

What special treat would you enjoy?

_____

_____

Cherish your memories. They are yours to keep and grow more precious over time.

Be patient with yourself. Allow yourself extra time to accomplish tasks.

Take time out for rest and relaxation. This will ease the stress of grief.

Most importantly, take your time and be gentle with yourself as you move through the holidays.

Holiday Traditions

With the loss of a member of your immediate family, holidays and special occasions will be difficult. Holidays are often filled with traditions and memories of closeness. As we face these days without our loved one, the empty space looms large in our hearts. By creating new traditions and understanding the common difficulties faced during the holidays, they can be easier to cope with.

AARP offers these tips in their article, "Frequently Asked Questions by the Widowed."

- ❏ Plan ahead. It helps to ease the strain.
- ❏ Set priorities. This can make it easier to phase out elements less pleasing to you.
- ❏ Make new traditions. This new phase in your life deserves some new traditions.
- ❏ Include [the deceased's] name in conversation. It helps others talk about him/her.

- Express your feelings. Most people understand and accept your need to cry.
- Find someone you can help. Giving assistance to others is very satisfying.
- Buy yourself something special. You've suffered a great loss. Be good to yourself.
- Cherish your memories. These are yours to keep; they grow more precious over time.
- Be patient with yourself. Allow yourself extra time to accomplish tasks.
- Take time out for rest and relaxation. This will ease the stress of grief.

Most importantly, take your time and be gentle with yourself as you move through the holidays.

Don't try to hold on to your previous traditions or the way things were done in the past. Your family has changed. It's okay to change the way you celebrate the holidays as well. Think of a new tradition. If you always celebrated Christmas at home, consider renting a cabin for a couple of days. If you always put up your tree early in the year, consider putting it up later. If a large dinner was always cooked, go out for dinner instead. Do things differently. The memories will be strong when the holidays come; altering routines is the best way to still find some joy.

Brook's family changed their routine after Caleb's death.

"Caleb died two months prior to Christmas. Both my mother and I had done most of our shopping. As Christmas neared and we were still heavily immersed in sadness, we wondered what to do with all the gifts. We decided to give them to Caleb's friends. To change our routine, instead of celebrating Christmas day at my mother's, she comes to my home. While we always have Caleb in our minds and hearts, we have learned the need to let go of some of the pain and engage in activities and new traditions that can help us move forward with our lives."

When we do what Brook has done, we are honoring our lost loved one. It may seem as though we are disrespecting our loved ones or moving away from our memories—but in fact, we are paying tribute by moving on with our lives.

Elizabeth was a newly widowed mother when the holidays came. She shares her story . . .

"The holidays, oh please save me from the holidays . . . make them go away! I remember my thoughts as a newly widowed mother of two young children sixteen years ago, as I raced around trying to put some kind of Thanksgiving and Christmas together. *Can't we just forget about it this year? Doesn't the rest of the world know how much pain I'm in?* I got together with another sad and lonely woman from my support group. I invited her and her kids to

my house to have a turkey dinner for Thanksgiving. It helped to not face the carving of the turkey (which he did, rather skillfully each year) alone. Somehow I did most of it, whatever "it" was, all the while listening to the happy Christmas carolers, fa la la la, la, la, la la.

Christmas day that first year was really strange. I opened the presents with my two children and then sat staring at the tree, imagining how it would feel to hurl the decorations off the deck and set the living room on fire. I must have sat in the green living room chair for two hours after that, not moving."

Where Does One Go During the Holidays?

Does one have to go anywhere? Do you have to pretend to be happy and joyous for the sake of others? Is it okay to celebrate this year if you want to? Like so much of the grief process, we need to listen to our inner guidance in these matters. If you need to be alone, that's okay. You can choose that. You may have to put something together for your kids and that's fine. You might find them a great joy and inspiration and a reason to get out of bed. Other than the practical needs of those who are dependent upon you, you don't need to take care of others by pretending "everything's all right."

If you do visit family and friends during the holidays, feel free to let them know the following ahead of time:

- I may need to leave your home earlier than you expect me to. (I get tired easily these days because I'm under a lot of stress.)
- I may need to take a walk by myself after dinner. (It's hard to be around happy families for too long a time.)
- I may cry unexpectedly when I hear certain music. (I have memories of good times and it's hard to hold back the tears.)
- I may not eat all the food and goodies you offer me. (My appetite hasn't been what it used to be—maybe I'm finding all this "hard to swallow.")

Even without a sudden death in your family or circle of friends, the holidays can bring up all kinds of difficult feelings. Depression is the most difficult feeling of all. You will need to face that it's going to be nearly impossible to stave off depression, especially at this time of year. Everyone seems to be so happy, families are gathering together, and there is a hole in your life. Walking through the mall you may see the perfect gift for your deceased loved one and dissolve into a flood of tears. You may have already bought the deceased gifts and there they sit, wrapped, under the tree, unopened. It would be extremely arrogant of us to suggest there is an easy fix for the kind of sadness that surfaces around the holidays. Both of us still suffer from periodic holiday blues. It may provide some relief to volunteer your time to help the needy and hungry. Giving of yourself to another, less fortunate person or to someone who has experienced a similar loss can take your mind off your own sadness—for a time.

This year, be one of the first people you think about during the holiday season. A support group will be especially useful during this trying time of year. Peers can offer rituals and ideas they use to make the holidays easier, or they can offer a shoulder to lean on in your time of need.

What special needs do you anticipate having this holiday season after reading this chapter? What can you do in advance to ease holiday stressors?

Chapter Eight
The Loss of a Friend

SUGGESTED READING:
I Wasn't Ready to Say Goodbye
Chapter 10: Losing a Friend

"There is only one way for you
To live without grief in your lifetime; that is
To exist without love. Your grief represents
Your humanness, just as your love does."
—*Carol Staudacher*

True, deep, abiding friends are hard to come by, and losing one, like all sudden losses, is extremely difficult to understand. Our connection to friends, newly hatched or life-long, may be more intimate than the connection we have to our families, or a family member may be the closest friend we have.

Many friends fulfill particular roles. A friend is rarely "just" a friend. Most friendships include elements of other relationships. For instance, in cases where we didn't have functional parenting, our friend may have become like a parent to us. In this case, the chapter where we discuss losing a parent will be additionally helpful to you. If your friend was much younger than you when he/she died, it may be that you served a parental role or were a significant mentor. Perhaps some of what is included in the chapter on losing a child will be helpful. If your friend was also your romantic love, the chapter on losing a significant other will give you some insights and support as you grapple with your loss. We hope this chapter will provide you with some useful ways to navigate the loss of a friend.

What roles did you play in your friend's life? What roles did he or she play in yours? Sibling? Were you a role model? Was he or she a mentor? Record the different roles below. Consider reading through these sections in the book and workbook for additional ideas and perspectives on the grieving process.

Reaching for the Phone—An Ongoing Dialogue

When a close friend dies suddenly, it is natural to feel cut off from your source of advice and companionship. Thrown into the ever-present reality of the moment, there you are with your questions, your fears, and your celebrations, and your friend isn't there to share them with you. In the past, your friend would have been beside you at a moment like this.

Consider keeping a notebook for an "Ongoing Dialogue" with your friend. Write down what you wish to say. Then imagine how your friend might respond. You may want to date these pages, as over time this can become a special journal of your friendship.

_____

_____

_____

_____

_____

_____

_____

_____

Close Ties

You might have been the loved one's confidant or closest person, or you may know the person better than anyone, but you are not formally or legally automatically included in the death process. This can be extremely challenging when you see families carrying out plans or rituals that contrast with what you believe your friend would have wanted.

Friendships tend to come and go throughout life, whereas family bonds are permanent. Even when families are estranged, a death often brings relatives together—at least for a time. If the family and friends of the family are not aware of your close friendship ties, you may find yourself grouped with "other caring people and well-wishers." You may feel the special closeness of your bond with the deceased is not understood or being respected.

It is important to remember in the aftermath of sudden death it is hard to care for one's self, let alone think clearly enough to keep everyone's best interest at heart. If the family is not aware of the depth of your friendship ties, it would be impossible for them to anticipate or consider your needs.

When Caleb died, Brook's mother Wendy was amazed by the number of friends Caleb had whom she had never met. She remembered many of the names from stories but hadn't realized how profoundly her son had impacted their lives. In the weeks, months, and even years following Caleb's death, it wasn't uncommon for one of his friends to stop by the house and introduce himself. Wendy loved these visits and hearing "Caleb stories" she had never heard before. By the time the friend would leave, both Wendy and the visitor had forged a new friendship based on their love for Caleb.

Consider paying a visit to one of the family members your friend spoke fondly about. Share stories and memories. This connection is likely to be valued and cherished by you and the family member. You may even emerge with a new friendship that cherishes your friend as the common bond.

Does the idea of reaching out to the family interest you? In what ways might you reach out? Offering to stop by? Sharing a story? A lunch invitation? Helping out with things-to-do? Sharing a holiday? Record your thoughts below.

_____

_____

_____

_____

_____

_____

_____

_____

_____

_____

Sharing Your Memories

Almost more than any other person, your relationship with the deceased was unique. He probably revealed to you more of his true nature than to anyone else, including his family. Your reminiscences and impressions of who he was will be more valuable because he was so real with you. In fact, you may know him better than his family because you spent more time with him over the years. What can you say? You can offer to share your stories. Brook's family found this extremely comforting.

"Caleb had more friends than anyone I've ever known. When he died, our house was flooded with his friends. My mother, Caleb's friends, and I would sit in our living room recalling memories and stories. We did this for days. We laughed together, we cried together, we grieved together.

Several of his closest friends had special stories they wanted to share. Some were funny, some were odd, and some were metaphysical. These friends offered to share their stories with us in private. We welcomed each story and my mother and I discuss them to this day. Do not be afraid to offer your story to a grieving family. Sharing our memories with one another is one of the best ways to keep our memories alive."

What stories do you have to share? How could you share them? Consider telling them directly, writing a story down as an essay, speaking a story into a recorder, or documenting your story in a memory book. This sharing can create a valuable memory for your friend's family and for you. When you need time to grieve, consider working on these stories.

Internalizing Your Friend

The loss of a friend takes an enormous toll on the soul. You may feel like their loss has taken a part of you away. One of the best ways to honor your friendship is to take some aspect of your friend's life or the way he lived his life and incorporate this part of his personality into who you are.

What traits did you admire most about your friend?

_____

_____

_____

_____

_____

_____

_____

In what ways could you incorporate these traits into your own life?

_____

_____

_____

_____

_____

_____

_____

Friend Support Group

Many support groups exist for those who have lost a partner or a child, but there are few that exist for the loss of a friend. One person that Pam knows formed a support group with the deceased's friends. This is a wonderful way to keep a friend's memory alive while working through grief.

Friends Support Group Invitation

The letter that follows is an example of a creative response to the need for support. The following invitational letter was written to family and friends by the deceased's sister, Karen. Kathleen's death was a suicide which occured after a long struggle with cancer and mental illness. The letter was written on stationary with this quote imprinted in the corner: "What we call the beginning is often the end. To make an end is to make a beginning. The end is where we start from." —T. S. Eliot

Dear Family and Friends,

During the past few weeks I have had the opportunity to speak with some of you regarding the impact of Kathleen's death on your life. These discussions have served to assist me in dealing with my grief.

Some of you mentioned that you've been so busy that you've hardly had time to feel, much less deal with the loss. Many societies throughout the world have rituals built into their communities to facilitate the difficult walk through grief. Our "progressive" society has only begun to realize it's shortcomings, and in efforts to counter the emotional isolation, society has assigned the task of assisting us with our grief work to counselors and mental health care (bereavement groups). These are valuable, however, I'd like to propose that another helpful way might be for the members of Kathleen's community come together to talk, sit, just be together, in an effort to promote healing.

The nature of Kathleen's death has left us all with many questions. In discussing these issues with some of you privately, it has come up that talking about the issues together may assist us all in finding peace.

I have enclosed information our family received from the Albany Medical Center the night Kathleen died. We have found it helpful to review this information regularly in an attempt to monitor our healing.

If Kathleen had been a participant in a hospice program, they would be offering a program for bereavement for the family and friends to have a framework to evaluate progress along the grief walk. Her mental illness was indeed terminal. In an effort to create a structure for us to walk in our grief I'd like to host the following afternoon gatherings.

Also, my family is trying to piece together a historical outline of Kathleen's life, birth to death. We would find it helpful to hear your experiences with Kathleen so we can add them to the tapestry we hope to create.

Thank you all for taking the time to call and talk. I look forward to further discussions and insights.

Schedule of Bereavement Gatherings:

3:00–5:00pm at 134 Ridge Avenue

(for those of you who wish to stay after, soup and sandwiches will be served)

Saturday, January 27—3 month anniversary of Kathleen's death

Saturday, April 27—6 month anniversary of Kathleen's death

Saturday, July 27—9 month anniversary of Kathleen's death

Saturday, October 26—1 Year

The first year of feeling the void and figuring out ways to compensate is the most difficult. If you cannot attend these gatherings, I would request that you make time to remember the memories.

I'd appreciate an RSVP call.

For those of you who experienced Kathleen's association with the Native American culture, you may recall her referring to their custom of communication to "all my relations." This demonstrates the understanding that we are all part of a network, a web, a community. When the fabric of the web is broken, loose ends flap around until the members can come together and mend the space. How we choose to repair the hole will depend on who we are and what we will bring to offer each other. Thank you all for your willingness to offer and obtain comfort. The hope is that the memories which cause pain in the initial blow can, in time, serve as great comforts and a means for our own growth.

Blessings to all.

In light and love,

Karen

Some Things You Can Do

Internalizing Your Friend

The loss of a friend takes an enormous toll on the soul. You may feel like their loss has taken a part of you away. One of the best ways to honor your friendship is to take some aspect of your friend's life or the way he lived his life and incorporate this part of his personality into who you are.

Contributions

Did your friend love children, lost animals, parks, the theater? Find an appropriate way to contribute time or money to an organization that promotes one of those special values.

Helping His Parents

If your friend was the child of aging parents who cannot drive, or who may not be able to care for the grave site, assure them you will, with fresh flowers, weeding, etc. From time to time, take a photo of the grave site to show them.

Friend Support Group

Many support groups exist for those who have lost a partner or a child, but there are few that exist for the loss of a friend. One person who Pam knows formed a support group with the deceased's friends. This is a wonderful way to keep a friend's memory alive while working through grief. We have included the letter this woman used to begin her group in the Appendix.

Which of these ideas could be of value to you?

_____

_____

_____

_____

_____

_____

_____

_____

_____

_____

_____

Chapter Nine
The Loss of a Parent

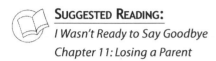

SUGGESTED READING:
I Wasn't Ready to Say Goodbye
Chapter 11: Losing a Parent

"...I learned to attend viewings even if I didn't know
the deceased, to press the moist hands
of the living, to look in their eyes and offer
sympathy, as though I understood loss even then.
I learned that whatever we say means nothing,
What anyone will remember is that we came..."
—*From the poem, "What I learned from My Mother" by Julia Kasdorf*

Many of us look to our parents for guidance and acceptance well into our adult lives. We rely on their opinions. We rely on them for our roots. When we lose a parent, a part of our history disappears. Whether we have a healthy relationship, are estranged from our parent, or have a parent who is unable to communicate as he or she once did due to health ailments, a loss of foundation still occurs. A link to our history is irrevocably lost.

How has your foundation been impacted by your loss?

_____

_____

_____

_____

_____

Even though we become adults, we do not stop being children. Our childhood needs, expectations, and yearnings are often masked by adult responsibilities and emotions, but the child still lives on within us. When we face the loss of a parent, those childhood needs often resurface. We grieve as both adult and child.

What does the child within you feel? How is the child within you grieving?

_____

_____

_____

_____

_____

_____

_____

_____

_____

_____

_____

_____

_____

_____

_____

_____

_____

Generation Shifts

In addition to the loss of foundation and emotional challenges we face, there are other challenges. For one, roles may shift. If we have lost our last living parent we move from the middle generation position (you are a child and you have children) to the older generation position.

Additionally, if you lose one parent suddenly, you may be left with the responsibility of caring for the surviving parent. Without warning or preparation, you must assume the role of caregiver. You become responsible for working with an attorney, the insurance company, maybe even a criminal trial in the courts.

What shifts have occurred from this loss?

_____

_____

_____

_____

_____

_____

_____

_____

_____

_____

_____

_____

_____

Grief . . . and Relief?

If your parents were elderly or in very poor health and you have been caring for them for some time, it is not uncommon to feel sadness mixed with relief. Feeling relief in the grief process can cause surviving children immense guilt. Know that it is okay to feel relieved that your parent is no longer in pain. It is also natural to feel relieved that the stress of day-to-day care has been lifted. These feelings do not mitigate or oppose your deep love for a parent. These are natural and healthy feelings after facing extremely challenging times.

If you have feelings you have been denying or suppressing because you fear they are not "acceptable," write them down. Let them out. Grief is a kaleidoscope of almost every emotion.

Regrets

If you and your parents were on the younger side (you in your twenties and they in their forties) at the time of death, you may have deep regrets over what you did and didn't get to do with them.

Do you have any regrets? Write them out and acknowledge them. Writing out these thoughts helps us to let them go. Holding onto them will block your grief work.

_____

_____

_____

_____

_____

_____

_____

_____

_____

_____

_____

_____

_____

_____

Words of Wisdom

Children look to their parents as mentors, often learning and seeking advice. Take a moment to think about the words of wisdom your parent might give you as you work your way through grief. Try to write down the words as they come to you. You can also try writing a specific question to your parent and then think about what they would write back and write it down.

Some Things You Can Do

Letter Writing

Write a letter to your parent expressing your true feelings and place it in the casket before burial or cremation. If the body was not recovered, you can burn the letter on a beach or some other outdoor place. As the smoke rises, imagine the words are being carried on the air to your parent.

Photographs

Find a photo of your parent that you have not yet framed. Take it to a photo store to be enlarged, have it framed, and hang it in a special place.

Listening

Keep "listening" for advice and guidance from your parent. Your parent may have died, but she was a powerful influence in your life. If what you "hear" is negative, now is the time to turn DOWN the volume on negative influences and turn UP the volume on positive influences.

Seek A Mentor

There may be someone else in your life that you can find who will help nurture and encourage you the way a good parent would. With the help of this surrogate parent, you may be able to get some of your unmet needs addressed.

Seek Out More Information

Talk to your parent's friends, work associates, or others involved in their daily activities and ask them to share stories of their times together.

Lessons Learned

Make a list of all you learned from your parent, good or bad. It can help to know that their life had meaning to you and that you received some very important life lessons from them. Even if your parent died an untimely death and was in your life for only a short time, you can surely find the meaning in your relationship. This can truly help you accept the loss and move on in your grief.

Which of these things could be of value to you?

Chapter Ten
The Loss of a Child

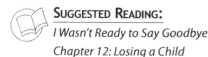

SUGGESTED READING:
I Wasn't Ready to Say Goodbye
Chapter 12: Losing a Child

"I've learned that I am much stronger than I ever gave myself credit for.
I've learned patience, because grief does not go away just because you want it to.
And I've learned that helping other people is sometimes the best help
I can give myself."
—*Donna F. Mother of a seventeen-year-old daughter who committed suicide*

It has been said that there is no loss as devastating as the loss of a child—regardless of your age or the child's. Sudden death is a mix-up of everything we know to be true in life. Losing a child to sudden death is a break in the natural law and order of life. The child we have spent our time loving and caring for and planning to watch well into adulthood has been taken. It is a heartbreak like no other. If the death was a suicide, the recovery is filled with another set of difficult emotions (see Chapter 13 on suicide). Those who live through and survive such an ordeal without becoming bitter have the strongest, most loving souls of all people walking the planet.

In her book, *Surviving Grief,* Doctor Catherine M. Sanders writes, "The reason parental grief is so different from other losses has to do with excess. Because loss of a child is such an unthinkable loss, everything is intensified, exaggerated, and lengthened. Guilt and anger are almost always present in every significant loss, but these emotions are inordinate with grieving parents. Experts estimate that it takes anywhere from three to five years to reach renewal after a spouse dies, but parental grief might go on for ten to twenty years or maybe a lifetime. Our lives are severely altered when our child dies and there can be no replacement. Substitutes offer little respite. This is not to say that there is no hope for happiness. It is just that the shock and severity of this kind of loss leaves us feeling completely helpless and full of dark despair."

As Dr. Sanders points out in the previous excerpt, our emotions are intensified with the loss of a child.

Extreme Emotions

There are so many dramatic changes and hardships to understand and overcome with the loss of a child. It has been said that after losing a child, we embark on a lifelong healing process. Understanding these unique challenges can help us to understand how to work through them.

Disorder

Disorder seems to be more prevalent after losing a child as compared to other losses. While we may face disorder in our physical and emotional lives, we also feel disorder within the world. When we have children, we expect them to outlive us. We build a future around our children. We build dreams and fantasies and goals. In short, we build a world. When a child is lost, these fantasies and dreams come crashing down without warning. Basic logic seems to have abandoned the world as we know it.

A Piece of Ourselves

Children are an extension of us. They carry many of our physical and personality traits forward into the world. We see ourselves in their eyes. Through our children, we envision a better future. When we lose a child, we lose this extension, and we lose this hope.

What piece of yourself or dream for the future did your child carry?

_____

_____

_____

_____

_____

_____

_____

_____

Guilt

Guilt runs strong in surviving parents. As a parent, we expect ourselves to be able to take care of our child. From birth, most parents promise their children they will protect them. When a child dies, we may feel a sense of personal failure. We may think we weren't "good enough" as parents. These distorted thoughts are the mind's attempt to make sense of the unfathomable.

If a close friend came to you and she had lost your child and then shared she was feeling guilty because of the thoughts you listed above, how would you advise her?

_____

_____

_____

_____

_____

_____

_____

_____

_____

_____

_____

_____

_____

_____

_____

_____

_____

_____

We are often much harder on ourselves than we are on anyone else. In the emotional times, try and treat your thoughts and feelings with the same kindness and encouragement you would your closest friend's.

Losing an Adult Child

Losing an adult child carries unique challenges. A parent has put so much time and energy into raising a child. You spend hours, days, and maybe years lecturing children on how to be safe. "Don't talk to strangers." "Stay away from drugs and alcohol." "Look both ways before crossing the street." After all this careful care and attention throughout their youth, you assume you are "out of the woods"—that now you will reap the rewards of watching your child develop as an adult. You wait for them to marry or follow a career or have children. When you lose a child at this life junction, although you have many precious memories, you are robbed of the future experiences you have expected.

In the brochure titled, *The Death of an Adult Child,* The Compassionate Friends write, "If the adult child dies as the result of an accident or an illness, parents are often told (while being comforted by friends or family) that they should be grateful that their child lived as long as he or she did. Of course you are grateful to have had your child for twenty-five, thirty, or forty years, but that does not mean your grief is lessened! Many parents have stated their relationship with the adult child had become one of friendship. They feel that they have not only lost their child, but a friend as well."

What mixed messages have you heard about grief? What mixed feelings are you having?

_____

_____

_____

_____

_____

_____

_____

For Parents with Surviving Children

In her book, *The Bereaved Parent*, Harriet Sarnoff Schiff touches on one of the hardest issues, that of grieving children. " . . . a recurrent theme appears to be that the living children received precious little by way of comfort from their parents."

Surviving children often feel their parents have abandoned them. A parent's grief is strong and often they cannot emotionally cope with the grief of their surviving children as well. This happens with many forms of loss, but when the loss is a child's sibling, the intensity is increased.

While you are engaged in acute grief, which will take at least a year, and for the loss of a child usually much longer, it's important to remember the perspective of your other children. Children are trying to cope with the loss of a sibling while also coping with an unfamiliar distance from their parents. It's important that surviving children understand that you are facing grief, and your behavior does not mean your love or feelings toward them have changed.

A common scenario after losing a child is an attempt to "make it right." Some parents will start an organization, fundraiser, or other memorial in the child's name. It is an admirable goal to keep the child's memory alive for generations to come. However, it is all too common for these memorials to become all-consuming. The parent spends so much time wrapped in the details of preserving his child's memory that he forgets to enjoy the children who are living!

Likewise, parents may constantly talk about the child who has died. Other children may quickly feel inferior, ignored, or unimportant if their parents focus so heavily on the other child. It is common to talk about the deceased frequently throughout the first six months to a year, but after that, there should be a point of letting go. While we can, of course, discuss emotions with friends or a counselor, within the family the letting go process has to take place if the current family unit is to remain healthy and intact. This doesn't mean that we forget. It means we begin to look toward the future and not dwell on the past. We bring balance into the home. We keep the memories of the past alive while creating new memories.

Have you been connecting with your other child(ren)? Are there any steps you can you take to reach out?

Your Relationship with Your Partner

The most intense challenge to the equilibrium of a relationship is the loss of a child. Studies have shown that married couples experience extreme stress during the three-year-period that follows the loss of a child.

Tonya lost her five-year-old son when he got in the crossfire of a robbery. She explains what she went through with her husband. "We were both so drained. It was like staring at each other through a thick fog—we kept trying to reach out to each other, knowing we needed each other, but we couldn't reach. He saw my pain and I saw his, and yet there was no energy to console each other."

Tonya's experience is a common one. A couple who previously worked as a team is left unable to function or help each other. The grieving process of couples is further complicated by history, gender differences, and expectations.

In his book, *When Goodbye is Forever: Learning to Live Again After the Loss of a Child*, John Bramblett shares his experiences after the death of his son. One story exemplifies the differences within a couple. In this story, he and his wife were at a Rotary party. While discussing unusual events surrounding his son's death with a small group of people, he noticed his wife staring at him through the sliding glass door. He writes, "I knew what she was thinking; she knew what I was talking about. I wanted to communicate my experience; it was part of my way of coping. She felt that talking about those striking episodes in our family's life cheapened them. Neither of us was wrong; our approaches were just different."

Understanding and respecting the differences in our individual grieving styles is necessary to work through grief together. Read through the chapter on the grieving styles of men and women for additional guidance.

Another complication is blame. If one parent was present when the death occurred, that parent may blame themselves or the other parent may blame them. Blame creates guilt, conflict, anger, and resentment. It is destructive and serves no purpose—yet it's a natural human emotion. In losses where one parent was present and blame occurs, seeking professional help is strongly advised. A third party to help navigate complex emotions is often needed.

What complications has grief brought to your relationship?

_____

_____

_____

_____

_____

_____

_____

_____

_____

Stay Connected

Even though you are wrapped in your unique grief, do not give up your connection as a couple. Make time to spend with each other. Don't shut each other out or you will be strangers when you get to the other side of grief. Schedule at least thirty minutes a day to sit together. Try and talk to each other about your feelings and the challenges of the day. If you can't talk about that, try talking about memories. If talking is too difficult right now, just hold hands or hold each other. This daily communication, whether physical or verbal, lets each partner know that the other is committed to working through the tragedy—together.

In what areas are you facing differences? List each difference and how you feel and your partner feels. What would be a compromise for both of you? Talk through this list with your partner.

_____

_____

_____

_____

_____

_____

_____

_____

Convey Your Needs

Miscommunication is the number one problem in any relationship—from work relationships to friendships to marriage. Don't let miscommunication further complicate your grieving process. Don't expect your partner to know what you need—tell him specifically. Likewise, don't assume that you know what your partner needs—ask him specifically.

Use one of the "My Needs" pages that follow to honestly and kindly write out the needs you have that you would like your partner to be aware of. Remember that one person cannot fulfill all of our needs. The ability to fulfill needs is lowered during times when emotional and physical energy is low. Do not think of this "needs list" as a list of demands, but rather think of it as things you would like your partner to know. Have your partner fill in the other page with his or her needs. Then discuss what you have both written, or exchange pages.

My needs include:

My needs include:

_____

_____

_____

_____

_____

_____

_____

_____

_____

_____

_____

_____

_____

_____

_____

_____

_____

_____

_____

_____

_____

_____

_____

Guidelines for Grieving Couples

Together, read the Loss of a Child and the Grieving Styles chapters from the *I Wasn't Ready to Say Goodbye* book.

It's important that you both understand grief and how it affects you as a couple. Read and discuss this chapter together. Use it as a springboard for questions such as, "Do you experience that?" or "Would you like to try that?"

Find Additional Support

One mistake that many married couples make is the expectation of having all their needs met by one person—their partner. This is unrealistic and puts too much pressure on a partner. Our needs are so diverse; it takes a diverse group of people to meet them. The same is true with grief. We need more than just our partner to help us through.

Discuss Issues Away from Home

The home environment will be charged with emotions and memories. To help overcome complicated emotions and distractions, make time to talk and share away from home. Take a break from the intensity of the situation. Go out for dinner, focus on one another, and talk through joys, problems, pains, and life.

Write Notes to Each Other

Therapist Tom Golden said, "I know a couple who has a terrible time talking about their grief but when they start writing notes to each other they gain a greater understanding. Give it a try." (Tom Golden maintains an excellent website, which has many articles on men and grief. *Tom Golden: Crisis, Grief & Healing.* See the Resources chapter for more information and the web address.) He also shares, "One way to give men more time is to write to them, rather than talk to them. By writing a note it gives the man the freedom to read it more than once, to take it with him . . . and [more] importantly to respond in his own time. Another benefit is that writing takes the non-verbal communication and the "tone of voice" out of the equation."

Convey Your Needs

Miscommunication is the number one problem in any relationship—from work relationships to friendships to marriage. Don't let miscommunications further complicate your grieving process. Don't expect your partner to know what you need—be specific. Try sentences that begin with "Here's what I need . . . " "Are you willing . . . "

Allow Time

It may take a while for men to articulate how they feel. Keep in mind that most men have not had as many opportunities to articulate their feelings in a safe environment as women have. If a woman asks a question, she needs to allow some time for the man to form his response. It could take minutes, hours, or even a day.

Ask Specific Questions

Men often aren't as familiar with their feelings and emotions as women. Questions like, "How are you feeling?" and "How are you doing?" are likely to be answered with, "Stop asking me," or "I'm all right." It's not that men are avoiding answering the questions, but rather they are simply answering them the way they always have. Women can try more specific questions for more specific answers. Questions like, "What was the hardest part of the funeral for you?" "What do you think John would want us to do today?" may help open the communication lines.

Listen, Listen, Listen

For men, the job of "just listening" can be incredibly challenging. Men hate to see others in pain—they think that they should be able to prevent or "solve" the pain of their wife or loved ones. But it's important to remember that women need someone who will just listen. Practice listening at every opportunity you have. For women, listening involves paying close attention to non-verbal communication, such as body language, as well.

Which of these guidelines could be of value to you?

_____

_____

_____

_____

_____

_____

_____

_____

Guidelines for Single Parents

The loss of a child carries unique challenges for the single parent. If the deceased was the only child, a single parent may find themselves living alone and the silence unbearable. There is no partner with whom to share the grieving process.

Perhaps the only challenge more difficult than the loss of a child is facing that loss alone. Yet that is the prospect faced by many single parents. For single parents, it is especially important to find a support network whether it be in-person or online (see the Appendix for online resources). Finding other parents who have survived the loss of their child will be a vital component in getting back on your feet. Also, it is common for the single parent to have a longer haul on the road of grief. What some people recover from in months may take years for the single parent. Be especially sensitive to your needs and emotions and seek the help of a professional or a support group.

Despite the difficulties in partner grieving, grieving alone also carries its own challenges. Couples have each other to lean on, despite their grieving differences. Single parents, however, are emotionally isolated. While they may have a network of friends, or rely on their ex-partner for a sense of support during tragedy, the life-partnership found in couples isn't present.

Find Support

Don't try to shoulder all the responsibilities on your own. Instead, seek out a network of friends and relatives to help you. As a single parent, you might be used to tackling tough issues alone—but the loss of a child is too much to face by yourself. Let yourself lean on friends and family who make themselves available.

Learn to Ask for Help

Because you have handled so many things alone, it can be difficult to ask for help. You will need to push yourself to reach out during these difficult times.

Remember Your Ex is Also Suffering

In the face of tragedy, try to put aside your differences with your "ex." Respect that you are both grieving the loss of your relationship with your child. One of you may have had a stronger relationship with your child, but that does not lessen the other parent's grief or make their grieving easier. Grieving for what "never was" is just as difficult as grieving for "what was"—perhaps even more difficult.

Living Children

Make sure to seek out another adult to help you care for surviving children during this time. They are experiencing their own grief, and it can be easy to lean on them for support (especially preteens and older). Children need their own space to grieve and a support network to do so.

Facing Your Loneliness

If you have lost your only child, you will likely experience a very intense sense of loneliness. At one point the title of "wife" or "husband" was taken from you, and now you may question your title as "mother" or "father." This is a very complicated mourning process and worthy of a book in itself. We strongly encourage you to seek out the help of a professional if you face this identity crisis. We want to emphasize that parenting cannot be taken from you. Once you are a parent—you are always a parent.

Which of these guidelines could be of value to you?

_____

_____

_____

_____

_____

_____

_____

_____

_____

_____

_____

_____

_____

_____

Chapter Eleven
The Loss of a Partner

 SUGGESTED READING:
I Wasn't Ready to Say Goodbye
Chapter 13: Losing a Partner

"Trying to put my pain behind brought me to many dead ends… Sometimes
I wondered if I was losing my mind. The old rules did not apply anymore.
I felt as if I had been dropped by parachute into a different country where
I had no map and everyone spoke a foreign language."
—*Cathleen L. Curry,* **When Your Spouse Dies**

The loss of a partner or spouse is devastating on many fronts. Our partner is often our confidant and best friend. We have both our emotional and physical highs and lows with this partner—day in and day out. To live without this "half" leaves us feeling incomplete, confused, and short-changed.

This is often intensified by the length of time we have spent with our partner. If we have been with our partner for many years, we may find that our partner completes our thoughts and is a compliment to our actions. We are left feeling as if we have lost half of our self in addition to our partner.

Added stressors arise at the life changes that often accompany the loss of a partner. We may have a significant financial change to endure, we may need to move, we may need to comfort our children, and have few people to comfort us.

Loss of Identity

Our partner makes up a significant portion of our history. With our partner, we interpret the world, daily events, and the ups and downs of life. When we lose this partner unexpectedly, we

126

lose many of the foundations of our identity. We are left to rebuild at a time when we are both emotionally and physically depleted. This rebuilding process will take time. Our friends and children may encourage us to move forward before we are ready. This is only to be expected, since those who care for us hate to see us in pain. Many people feel that by "getting back into life," our pain will be alleviated. These are good intentions, but this route does not work in reality.

As we grieve, we will need to rebuild our foundation, one brick at a time. In his book, *Loss*, John Bowlby writes, "Because it is necessary to discard old patterns of thinking, feeling and acting before new ones can be fashioned, it is almost inevitable that a bereaved person should at times despair that anything can be salvaged and, as a result, fall into depression and apathy. Nevertheless, if all goes well, this phase may soon begin to alternate with a phase during which the bereaved starts to examine the new situation and to consider ways of meeting it. This redefinition of self and situation is as painful as it is crucial, if only because it means relinquishing all hope that the lost person can be recovered and the old situation re-established. Yet until redefinition is achieved no plans for the future can be made."

At first, nothing will feel comfortable. Each day will bring new realizations and troubles. But in time, you'll find yourself engaging in a memory or hobby or thought that you enjoy. It may be only a minute of "peace," but peace nonetheless. This becomes your first brick. Seek out these sources of peace and record them in a journal. Notice what you like and what you don't. Form new opinions. Pursue a new interest. You may not be able to move quickly on these things. You may want to take a "getaway," but not have the emotional energy. That's fine. Order a few travel brochures on the Internet and page through them. A step is a step—no matter how small.

Write about the role you had prior to your loss and how that role has changed. What do you feel about it? Are you scared? Angry? Let your feelings flow.

_____

_____

_____

_____

_____

_____

_____

Incorporate Traits

Incorporate some special trait or behavior of your deceased partner into your own life so that every time you exhibit that trait or behavior, you will be honoring the loved one's memory.

What traits, characteristics, or qualities do you remember or admire most?

_____

_____

_____

_____

_____

How can you incorporate one of these traits into your daily life?

_____

_____

_____

_____

_____

_____

_____

_____

_____

_____

Love Letters

Many widows and widowers have reported letter writing to be a valuable way to release their emotions and remember their loved one. Begin a notebook and write a letter whenever the urge strikes. Release your emotions, your thoughts, your words.

One of Pam's clients, the husband of a woman who died in a skiing accident, keeps a "love letter journal" where he writes to his wife each day. There will come a day when he doesn't do this at all, or as much, but for now this gives him a great deal of comfort.

Use the space below to write a letter to your partner.

Dear _____ ,

_____

_____

_____

_____

_____

_____

_____

_____

_____

_____

_____

_____

If You Still Have Children in the Home . . .

Additional Responsibilities

After a mother or father has died, one parent becomes the key decision maker and responsible person for the children. He or she will be in charge of decisions on college, finances, rules, curfews, limits, and all other responsibilities. Both parent and child will need time to adapt to these new roles.

Involving children in restructuring the home is one idea that many parents have found helpful. This works best with children who are ten and older. A month or two after the services, explain to them that with one less family member, your family will need to use teamwork and cooperation. Offer ideas on how you think the family could run smoothly. Brainstorm ideas beforehand. Try things like chore distribution, helping with dinner, doing something together as a family on one day each weekend, etc. It may seem hard to be talking of functionality so soon after losing someone, but although someone's life has stopped, our lives don't.

In what ways has your loss impacted your routines and home life? What specific routines need to be restructured? How can your children help?

_____

_____

_____

_____

_____

_____

_____

_____

_____

_____

_____

Structure

Children need a stable base in order to thrive. Part of creating a stable base is consistency, boundaries, and limit setting. Often, we are so emotionally depleted that maintaining consistency and boundaries is challenging at best. Keep things as regular as you are able. This will help children find a safe, stable environment in which to grieve.

What can you do to increase stability? What boundaries can you keep? (Bedtimes, meal times, rules, etc.)

_____

_____

_____

_____

_____

_____

_____

_____

_____

_____

_____

_____

_____

_____

Some Things You Can Do

As you move on with your life, remember this: The love you have for your deceased partner will always have a special place in your heart and history, even if/when you have another love relationship and/or remarry. Buy a special box for your momentos and revisit this box on special days if you want to.

Donate

Donate time, money, or special items to a charity that was important to your deceased partner.

Incorporate Traits

Incorporate some special trait or behavior of your deceased partner into your own life so that every time you exhibit that trait or behavior, you will be honoring the loved one's memory.

Write Letters

Many widows and widowers have reported letter writing to be a valuable way to release their emotions and remember their loved one. Begin a notebook and write a letter whenever the urge strikes. Release your emotions, your thoughts, your words.

One of Pam's clients, the husband of a woman who died in a skiing accident, keeps a "love letter journal" where he writes to his wife each day. There will come a day when he doesn't do this at all, or as much, but for now this gives him a great deal of comfort.

Place an Ad

Place an "In Memory Of" ad in your local paper, in remembrance of your deceased partner and have it signify the closing of one phase of your life and the beginning of another. The ad can contain a favorite poem, song lyrics, special graphics, or thoughts about your deceased partner. You can choose any date that was meaningful to both of you.

Read the section on holidays, anniversaries, and other difficult days. Look for ways to honor your loved one routinely throughout the year.

Which of these guidelines could be of value to you?

_____

_____

_____

_____

Chapter Twelve
The Loss of a Sibling

 SUGGESTED READING:
I Wasn't Ready to Say Goodbye
Chapter 14: Losing a Sibling

> "My big brother was so good to me.
> When we were kids, he always let me go first.
> The night he died, he looked up at me,
> Smiled his little crooked smile, and said,
> 'Sis, this time let me go first.'"
> —*Connie Danson, eulogy for her brother, Frank Darnell*

No matter your ages at the time of death, the loss of a sibling carries many unique challenges. First and foremost, when we lose our sibling, we lose one of the people who knows us most intimately. This person grew up as we grew. We laughed together, schemed together, cried together, fought with each other, hated each other, and loved each other. It is one of the only relationships that experiences, and endures, such a full spectrum of emotions day after day.

In *The Worst Loss*, Barbara D. Rosof writes of siblings: "They are playmates, confidants, competitors; they may also be protectors, tormentors, or have special responsibilities. Siblings know each other more intimately than anyone else. Siblings know, as no one else in the world does, what it is like to grow up in your particular family. Relationships with a brother or sister help children know who they are and how they fit in the family. The bonds between siblings are woven into the fabric of each one's life."

When we lose a sibling, we lose a piece of ourselves, a piece of our family, and a reflection of ourselves. We lose a precious link to our history and an ally in our future.

Being Overlooked in the Grieving Process

One of the hardest parts of sibling loss is being overlooked in the grieving process. A person can find evidence of this by opening the many books on grieving in a bookstore. Pages upon pages are devoted to parents and spouses. However, the loss of a sibling is not listed as often—and when it is, the coverage is often short. For the Resources section of this book, we had a hard time finding anything geared specifically to sibling loss. One young adult who lost his sister wondered why everyone always asked, "Well how are your parents taking it?" and never asked how *he* was taking it. An article in the *Journal News* titled, "Forgotten Mourners" offered the views of many surviving siblings. One person quoted in the article said, " . . . I was so mad. It was as if everyone thinks, *Oh my gosh, losing a child, that's the worst thing in the world,* and they don't even consider there are siblings."

Have you felt overlooked in the grieving process? By whom and how so?

Double the Loss

In addition to losing a sibling, the surviving brothers or sisters often lose a piece of their parents. Parents become wrapped in their grief. For years to come, they may have difficulty relating like before with the surviving children. Many of these surviving siblings don't feel they can go to their parents. "My father had enough on his mind," said one man we interviewed, who sadly watched his relationship with his father deteriorate. One thirty-five-year-old woman named Lee said this in the *Journal News* article, "I don't think society understands what sibling grief is all about. It's a misunderstood grief because it's a double-edged sword. You have your own pain and your parents' pain."

Have you felt that in addition to the loss of your sibling, you have lost part of the relationship you previously had with one or both of your parents? Write about how things have changed.

_____

_____

_____

_____

_____

_____

_____

_____

_____

_____

_____

_____

_____

_____

_____

_____

_____

_____

_____

Role Reversal

After the death of a sibling, it is not uncommon to see a role-reversal between parent and child. The surviving sibling may feel a push to step in and support the parent emotionally and/or financially. A parent may lean on a child in new ways (no matter what the age of the child). Have the roles of your relationship changed? How does that make you feel?

_____

_____

_____

_____

_____

_____

Are there any roles now missing in your life? Do you need to seek support from others to fulfill roles that are no longer occupied by your parent? Who can you turn to for support?

_____

_____

_____

_____

_____

_____

_____

_____

Survival-Living

In the initial months following a loss, all any of us can do is attempt to navigate grief's path as much as possible. The world is not perfect, nor are we. We often make decisions that are focused more on getting by day to day than on thinking long term. Somewhere between the second and twelfth month, we begin to shift back to longer-term thinking and are often surprised to find many of our relationships have changed. There is a tendency to blame this on grief. Usually grief played a part—it catapulted us into a new world in which we thought differently and were concerned more with day-to-day survival than long-term quality of life. Each of us lives this day-to-day survival life for a different length of time, depending on our previous experience with grief, our support network, the level of shock, how present the loved one was in our day-to-day life, and our ability to grieve in healthy ways.

When one person is living day to day and another is not, a gap forms in the relationship. The person thinking day to day may not have the emotional energy or foresight to think of anything or anyone besides that with which they physically come into contact. The longer two individuals remain on different tracks, the wider the gap in the relationship can become.

After the death of a loved one, the gap widens when both parent and surviving children go into shock and survival living. The parent often has the widest network. Energies of supporters are often focused primarily on helping the parent, which can (doesn't always) enable the pattern of "survival living" for a longer period. The surviving sibling often has little support. Without support, the surviving sibling will move back to longer-term thinking/living more quickly in an attempt to support himself or find support elsewhere. The parent continues in this survival-living mode for a couple of months or half a year or more. The parent becomes accustomed to focusing only on challenges right in front of them. The surviving sibling is no longer living with their parent and not "right in front of them." The surviving sibling feels isolated, lost, and alone. Meanwhile, the parent has lost all track of time. Because the parent has people coming to her recognizing and validating her loss in this unfamiliar territory, she does not realize that the surviving sibling is grieving alone.

Can you see this cycle in your relationship with one of both parents? How so?

_____

_____

_____

_____

_____

_____

_____

_____

_____

_____

Don't Let the Gap Grow

If a gap exists in your relationships, it is important to articulate it and take steps to close the gap, or it will continue to grow. You may feel that your parent should reach out to you, but this expectation will not help matters or solve the problem. If you were close with your parent before, then seek to restore the relationship.

Take a moment to write down what you miss the most about how your relationship was before.

_____

_____

_____

_____

_____

_____

_____

_____

If we go to our parent and are accusing or negative, we only compound his or her pain and ours. What are some specific, healthy ways you can restore some of the relationship qualities you miss? For example, could you meet for lunch or go to a movie?

_____

_____

_____

_____

_____

_____

_____

_____

_____

_____

_____

_____

_____

During these times, keep the majority of the conversation about you or the parent—not the loss of your sibling. Set aside other times to talk about the loss. Try and develop a routine—for example, talk about the loss when you are at your parent's house, but when in public, try to direct the conversation toward you or the parent. You do not need to share this routine or intention with your parent, just use it as a guideline for yourself to restore a healthy relationship. In time, your parent will likely follow your lead and adapt.

While we cannot hold back grief with rigid boundaries, we can guide it. Guiding it with specific times for grief-talk and specific times for parent/child talk can help everyone get their needs met. In this fashion, we can honor our loved one yet also honor each other equally.

Forgiving a Parent or Parents

If your parents were unavailable to you when you experienced your grief, or if they didn't know how to help you through it, it's important to forgive them. When we hold onto angry feelings, we don't leave the room needed to heal. One effective way to forgive is to write a letter. Explore all your feelings on paper. Write out your anger, your fears, and your hopes. When you finish, put the paper in a drawer. Periodically over the next month, pull it out and read it. Feel the pain that you experienced. After a month, add a note of forgiveness to your parents. Then burn the letter and let your feelings of anger rise with the smoke.

Use this space to write a letter to your parent(s) expressing your feelings.

_____

_____

_____

_____

_____

_____

_____

_____

_____

_____

_____

_____

_____

In a month or so, come back and re-read your letter. Then write a letter of forgiveness below.

When People Idealize Your Sibling

If parents begin to idealize the deceased child, a surviving child's feelings of pain. Idealization involves seeing what we want to see versus reality. It is often used in grief to try and ease pain or to make a memory stronger or more solid. Examples of idealization might be a parent saying things like, "She was an angel. She was taken early because she was too precious for this world." While these are seemingly innocent statements, as a surviving sibling you might think, *Does that mean I am not precious, that is why I am here?* Perhaps you know otherwise because of your close relationship to your sibling, and you can see through this statement, but out of respect, you do not say anything. A parent may also "forget" the annoyances and challenges she faced with your sibling and focus on only the strengths and joys. This can create an incredibly high bar for any surviving sibling and a feeling of resentment toward the grieving parent.

In the book, *When a Friend Dies,* Marilyn E. Gootman writes, "Sometimes people are afraid to say anything bad about someone who has died. They turn the dead person into a saint. Every person in this world has strong points and weak points, even those who have died. Loving someone means being honest and accepting the whole person, both the good and the bad, even if the person is dead."

Who have you seen idealize your sibling? What have they specifically said? Write down each person and the statement. Then write how the statement made you feel. Often putting these realizations on paper causes anger. Discuss these statements with a close friend or use the strategies in this workbook for processing anger. When we get our anger outside of our mind, we can work with it. When it remains lodged within us, it becomes a block to healing.

Hot and Cold Nature of Sibling Relationships

Sibling rivalry is a natural part of growing up. In some families it's exaggerated, and in others it's practically nonexistent. You may have fought with your sibling, said terrible things, or thought terrible thoughts. No matter how crazy, outrageous, or hateful these things seem to you—be assured, this is *natural.* Inside our guilt, we magnify these bad times—we narrow in on our regrets. There is no need to do this. One way siblings learn about one another and their place in the world is through these rivalries. For each rivalry you focus on, remember a wonderful shared moment, no matter how small or how simple.

Siblings often have a love-hate relationship until well into adulthood. While still kids, it's not uncommon to be best friends one minute and worst enemies the next. This double-sided relationship often complicates the grief process. You may find yourself wishing you had been nicer, more forgiving, or less jealous. Blame and guilt can reign strong for surviving children. Grief exaggerates both the positive and negative of any relationship. Because the relationship can no longer evolve or change, it is frozen in time and we tend to hone in on specific moments in a way we would not do with those who are living.

Are you being critical of yourself for certain moments of your sibling relationship? Record these moments below.

Imagine if you were to try and hone in on the specific moments of *all* your important relationships. You will likely be able to quickly see that placing relationships under a microscope is not practical or purposeful. Relationships are not comprised of individual one-time moments, but rather a garland of moments over time. If we pick out specific moments, we disrupt the entire garland. Focus on the whole and not the individual parts.

Write a few paragraphs about the "whole" of your relationship. If you are stuck, try the following sentence starter: *Our sibling relationship was unique and special because . . .*

_____

_____

_____

_____

_____

_____

_____

_____

_____

_____

_____

_____

_____

_____

_____

_____

_____

Identity through a Sibling

Siblings define one another. We become "Joe's sister" or "Frank's brother." It's common for a sibling to also explain themselves in relationship to their deceased sibling, or a parent (i.e. "I act more like my mother and my brother has my father's traits.") When we lose our sibling this identity is taken from us. Within familiar environments where we are known as "Joe's sister" or "Frank's brother," a bittersweet memory remains.

How has your identity changed through your loss? How will that change in identity impact relationships you have with others? How does that change in identity impact the relationship you have with yourself?

Additionally our birth order is altered. Mothers Against Drunk Driving offers the following in their brochure, **WE HURT TOO.** "When a brother or sister dies, you now experience a gap in the birth order. If the oldest sibling was killed, the second oldest is now the oldest. If there were just the two of you, you are now an 'only child.' It is difficult to know whether or not you should try to assume a new role, but you are painfully aware of the void left by your sibling's death."

At this point in the grieving process, do not concern yourself with a new role or whether you should assume one. Do, however, recognize the gap that now exists. Write down what roles have changed. For example, if you were one of two children, you might write, "I am now an only-adult child." If you were the middle child, you might write, "I was once a middle child, now I am the youngest (or oldest)."

Words of Wisdom

In *The Worst Loss,* Barbara D. Rosof writes of siblings: "They are playmates, confidants, competitors; they may also be protectors, tormentors or have special responsibilities. Siblings know each other more intimately than anyone else. Siblings know, as no one else in the world does, what it is like to grow up in your particular family. Relationships with a brother or sister help children know who they are and how they fit in the family. The bonds between siblings are woven into the fabric of each one's life."

Siblings often give words of wisdom to one another (albeit sometimes smart-alec advice instead of sensitive advice). The closeness of a sibling relationship allows siblings to see one another in unique ways. Take a moment to think about the words of wisdom your sibling might give you as you work your way through grief. Try to write down the words as they come to you. You can also try writing a specific question to your sibling and then think about what they would write back and write it down.

_____

_____

_____

_____

_____

_____

_____

_____

_____

_____

_____

Some Things You Can Do

Forgiveness

If your relationship with your sibling was challenging or pain-filled, it is important to heal and let go. When we hold onto angry feelings, we don't leave the room needed to heal. One effective way to forgive is to write a letter. Explore all your feelings on paper. Write out your anger, your fears, and your hopes. When you finish, put the paper in a drawer. Periodically over the next month, pull it out and read it. Feel the pain that you experienced. After a month, add a note of forgiveness To your sibling. Then burn the letter and let your feelings of anger rise with the smoke.

"Communicate" with Your Sibling

In your mind, talk to your sibling like you always did. No matter what your relationship with your sibling—good or bad—you are bound to be tied by the closeness of growing up together in a family. Talk to your sibling and internalize his spirit. When you have a question or doubt, find a quiet place and think about your sibling and what advice he might have given you.

A Memory Notebook

Consider keeping a notebook for memories, cherished moments, and times together throughout the years. When you are seeking time with your sibling, work in this memory notebook. You may want to list ages at the top of the pages—for example have one page for when you were two and your sibling was five, another couple of pages for when you were three and your sibling was six. Leave more pages for the years where you have more memories.

Getaway for a While

Take a weekend getaway to explore your grief. Often we don't want to share our strong emotions with our parents or partners. If we are married, we may feel like we are putting too much on the shoulders of our spouse or children by sharing with them. A weekend where you need only worry about yourself, and not day-to-day demands can be especially cleansing and self-nurturing. Take with you a journal and this book and work on some of the exercises. Take long walks outside and "commune" with your sibling.

Which of these guidelines could be of value to you?

Chapter Thirteen
When Loss is from Suicide

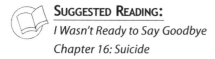

SUGGESTED READING:
I Wasn't Ready to Say Goodbye
Chapter 16: Suicide

"Gradually, I came to understand that while it may be
possible to help someone whose fear is death, there are no
guarantees for a person whose fear is life."
—*Carla Fine*

Over 90 percent of people who die by suicide have a mental illness at the time of their death. According to a study released by the Centers for Disease Control and the National Institute for Mental Health, suicide is the eleventh leading cause of death in the U.S., with 32,000 deaths recorded in 2004 and over 800,000 attempts. This approximates to around one death every sixteen minutes. Each year in the United States, there are more suicides than homicides. From 1952 to 1992, the incidence of suicide among teens and young adults tripled. Today, it is the third-leading cause of death among youth (after motor vehicle accidents and unintentional injury).

A U.S. Centers for Disease Control survey of high-school students showed that 34 percent of girls and 21 percent of boys have considered suicide, actually *during the last year* 16 percent of high-schoolers made a "specific plan," and 8 percent "tried suicide" .

Suicide is one of the most devastating types of loss. In her book *How to Go On Living When Someone You Love Dies,* Therese A Rando, PhD, writes, "This can contribute to a profound shattering of your self-esteem, with strong feelings of unworthiness, inadequacy, and failure. Like homicide, this death was not inevitable. It was preventable. You must recognize that you are particularly victimized by this type of death, and are susceptible to intensified and conflicted bereavement reactions."

But we are not at fault for someone's suicide. In the end, in the final moment, they made the choice alone. In *No Time to Say Goodbye: Surviving the Suicide of a Love One,* Carla Fine writes,

"Like most survivors, I was haunted by the infinite regrets that are woven into the fabric of suicide. I would replay the chronology of events leading up to Harry's death, searching for lost opportunities to reverse the inevitable outcome. Only as I began to accept the idea that my husband's choice to kill himself was his alone did the powerful grip of "what-ifs" of his suicide begin to loosen. Gradually, I came to understand that while it may be possible to help someone whose fear is death, there are no guarantees for a person whose fear is life."

Write about your feelings about suicide. What did you believe prior to surviving the suicide of a loved one? What do you believe now? What questions do you have? Getting your feelings on paper is the first step in dealing with them.

Common Reactions to Suicide

Shock, Guilt, Grief, Anger, Depression, and Denial

When someone commits suicide shock, guilt, grief, anger, depression, and denial work overtime. In the minds of many people, suicide is seen as a *preventable* . With this being the case, many survivors feel intense guilt and anger, since they were unable to prevent the suicide. When the one who has died is your child, the emotions intensify further. The Compassionate Friends write, "The suicide of one's child raises painful questions, doubts, and fears. The knowledge that your love was not enough to save your child and the fear that others will judge you to be an unfit parent may raise powerful feelings of failure. Realize that as a parent you gave your child your humanness—your positives and negatives— and that what your child did with them was primarily your child's decision."

Questions and Suicide

The question that survivors of suicide ask over and over again is "*why?*" "Why would he (or she) take his life?" The "need to know" feelings are intensified when suicide occurs. The Mental Health Association in Waukesha County, Wisconsin, published a pamphlet titled *Grief after Suicide*, which states: "Why would anyone willingly hasten or cause his or her own death? Mental health professionals who have been searching for years for an answer to that question generally agree that people who took their own lives felt trapped by what they saw as a hopeless situation. Whatever the reality, whatever the emotional support provided, they felt isolated and cut off from life, friendships, etc. Even if no physical illness was present, suicide victims felt intense pain, anguish, and hopelessness. John Hewett, author of *After Suicide*, says, 'He or she probably wasn't choosing death as much as choosing to end this unbearable pain.'"

While you will never know the complete thought processes of the person who took his or her own life, know that you are not alone in your questioning. Many support groups, both in-person and online can help you explore your questions and feelings. Please see the Resources chapter for support ideas.

What questions do you have about suicide? Who could help answer them?

_____

_____

_____

Religion and Suicide

There are many mixed emotions, thoughts, and feelings on suicide and religion. For those affiliated with churches that take a harsh view of suicide, this can be an especially difficult time. In Eva Shaw's book, *What to Do When A Loved One Dies*, she writes: "While suicide is mentioned throughout the Bible's Old Testament, there is no opinion, condemnation, or condoning. Saint Augustine said it was a grievous sin and the Catholic church and a few Protestant denominations have, at times, taken a harsh view of suicide. All major religions have abolished the philosophy that suicide is a cardinal sin, however, you may have to forgive [or ignore] a few people who make comments about the religious aspect of suicide."

The Compassionate Friends offer the following on the topic of suicide, "Cultural and religious interpretations of an earlier day are responsible for the stigma associated with suicide. It is important that you confront the word *suicide*, difficult as it may be. Keeping the cause of death a secret will deprive you of the joy of speaking about your child and may isolate you from family and friends who want to support you. Rather than being concerned about the stigma surrounding suicide, concentrate on your own healing and survival. Many parents prefer to use the phrase "completed suicide" rather than the harsh "committed suicide" when speaking about their child."

The people around us may also have a hard time understanding and accepting suicide. Therese A. Rando, PhD, writes, "The normal need to know why the death occurred will be intensified in suicide." You will need to work hard at answering the questions in your own mind, so that when you are ready, you can talk to others about your child comfortably.

If you have lost someone from suicide, get more information. The Internet has many valuable resources and online support forums; additionally, many books are devoted to the topic. If you are comfortable in a support group setting, there are many for suicide survivors. Check the Resources chapter or call your local church, hospital, or college for ideas on local groups. You will need to come to a point where you can remember your lost loved one realistically—both the positives and the negatives.

The poem on the following page offers a beautiful perspective and ode to those we have lost from suicide.

Tattered Kaddish
by Adrienne Rich

Taurean reaper of the wild apple field
messenger from earthmire gleaming
transcripts of fog
in the nineteenth year and the eleventh month
speak your tattered Kaddish for all suicides:

Praise to life though it crumbled in like a tunnel
on ones we knew and loved

Praise to life though its windows blew shut
on the breathing-room of ones we knew and loved

Praise to life though ones we knew and loved
loved it badly, too well, and not enough

Praise to life though it tightened like a knot
on the hearts of ones we thought we knew loved us

Praise to life giving room and reason
to ones we knew and loved who felt unpraisable

Praise to them, how they loved it, when they could.

Singing Lessons

In *Singing Lessons,* author Judy Collins writes about her personal journey of recovery after her son Clark's suicide . . . "On the anniversary of Clark's death, I woke from a dream at midnight. In my dream I had been trying to persuade Clark not to die—striving to convince him that he didn't have to die, he didn't have to end his life. My son smiled and looked at me with love in his eyes. 'Mother . . .' he said, 'death is not an ending.'

Today, I don't have to stay in depression. I know I have tools:

- I read a spiritual book.
- I call a friend who has a kind word, a lift in her voice.
- I think about the good things in my life—often writing them down. There is so much in my life for which to be grateful.
- I smile with my husband, my friends, my mother, and my sister.
- In the moment of silence, there is the sound of God bringing me strength—bringing me healing."

What tools do you have to help you in your journey through grief?

_____

_____

Some Things You Can Do

- Learn as much as you can about suicide, especially the myths. Understanding the facts can help relieve guilt.
- If you discovered your loved one, be acutely aware of the possibility of Post-Traumatic Stress Disorder. Consider talking with a mental health professional.
- Write out on paper your thoughts, questions, and anger. When we keep our complex emotions locked within, we further torment ourselves. Make time daily to "let it out."
- Find others, either online or in person, who have lost a loved one to suicide. Ask questions. Find guidance and strength from those who have survived this path before you.
- Confront the reality of life. We are all human. There are things we tried to do and there are things we did not do. In hindsight we often see only the things we did not do or "missed signs." We cannot do everything for everyone. We cannot see the future. We cannot know that recognizing the "missed signs" or doing things we did not do would have changed the outcome.
- If guilt is plaguing you, write down specifically what you feel guilty about. Write a letter to your loved one sharing the truth and intensity of your guilt. Write another letter back to yourself offering forgiveness.
- Remember you did not have a choice about or control over your loved one's decision to commit suicide. However, you do have control over how to live your life today and going forward.

Chapter Fourteen
Additional Exercises for Your Journey

SUGGESTED READING:
I Wasn't Ready to Say Goodbye
Chapter 19: The Road Ahead
Chapter 21: Self-Help and Therapy Chapter 22: The Grief Recovery Process
Appendix II: Grief Resources and Support

> "Let us turn over the page
> And see what is written
> On the other side of the night."
> —*Thomas McGrath, from "Graveyard Shift"*

The exercises within this chapter cover a wide variety of situations and emotions. Read through them, finding those that pertain to your unique loss or those that will offer you comfort and growth.

Internalizing Our Loved One

The loss of a loved one takes an enormous toll on the soul. You may feel like their loss has taken a part of you away. One of the best ways to honor your relationship is to take some aspect of your loved one's life or the way he lived his life and incorporate this part of his personality into who you are.

Write about the traits you admired in your loved one. Choose one that you feel you could integrate into your personality as a tribute.

_____

_____

_____

_____

_____

_____

_____

_____

_____

_____

_____

Contributions in the Name of Someone You Love

Did your friend love children, lost animals, parks, the theater? Find an appropriate way to contribute time or money to an organization that promotes one of those special values.

List any organizations you would like to research.

_____

_____

_____

_____

_____

_____

_____

Helping Parents

If your loved one has aging parents who cannot drive, or who may not be able to care for the grave site, assure them you will, with fresh flowers, weeding, etc. From time to time, take a photo of the grave site to show them.

What tasks might the parents need help with? What can you commit to helping with? Are there other people that you can solicit help from as well?

_____

_____

_____

_____

_____

_____

_____

_____

_____

_____

_____

_____

_____

_____

_____

Letter Writing Exercise

Write a letter to your loved one expressing your true feelings and place it in the casket before burial or cremation. If the body was not recovered, (or you are doing this exercise after the service) you can burn the letter on a beach or some other outdoor place. As the smoke rises, imagine the words are being carried on the air to your loved one.

Other Ideas to Honor Someone Who Has Died

Develop a Living Memorial

Many parents find comfort in developing a memorial, informational pamphlet, or organization in their child's name. In our interviews we have found parents who have published information on drunk driving, drug use, suicide, gangs, etc. and distributed it in their local community, or sent it to newspapers around the country. Other parents have developed or founded organizations that are now national in scope. Other parents have found peace in starting a scholarship fund in their child's name and awarding the scholarship to a child who wants to pursue an interest similar to their child. Brook's family started an annual water-ski tournament in her brother's honor. Caleb was a nationally-recognized water skier who enjoyed tournament skiing. Each year, they hold a tournament at the lake at which Caleb loved to ski and award cash prizes and plaques.

International Star Registry

We discovered this group and thought the idea was precious. "Honor your loved one by giving them the stars! What a beautiful way to memorialize your child by naming a star after him or her! Since 1979, the International Star Registry has been bringing these dreams to earth by offering a unique and magical opportunity to name a star. Plus, when you purchase your star through MISS, a portion of the proceeds will be donated directly to the combined efforts of MISS and the Arizona SIDS Alliance." The star kit includes a certificate, a telescope coordinated for locating the named star, a large sky chart with the star circled for easy identification, an astronomy booklet and a memorial letter. The price ranges from $57 to $106, including shipping and handling. For more information, write to MISS/Star Registry, 8448 W Aster Dr., Peoria, AZ 85381 or visit the website online at www.misschildren.org/family/starreg.html.

Donations

In her book, *A Handbook for the Living as Someone Dies*, Elizabeth A. Johnson suggests, "It may be very therapeutic and rewarding for you to donate your child's toys and other belongings to a children's home or to the children's wing at a hospital or hospice. In this way, the energy of your child's possessions is passed onto other children. A part of him continues to brighten the lives of others."

Memory Books

Creating a memory book is a wonderful keepsake of our loved one. When Brook's brother died, she collected articles, photos, and other memorabilia to put in a keepsake album. Using different papers, stencils, markers, and stickers she created special pages to "frame" her memories.

Album making has become popular in recent years. Many scrapbooking stores now exist that offer classes on how to archive our memories creatively. Through collage, rubber stamping, paper decorations, and other means, we can make a beautiful book to serve as a remembrance.

In addition to stores that can serve as creative outlets, many magazines and books offer guidance. Even if you don't consider yourself creative, there are tools to help you get started. Check the craft section of your local bookstore for books on scrapbooking. A large newsstand or craft store may carry magazines such as *Memory Makers* and *Somerset Studio,* which offer ideas.

There are also consultants for companies like D.O.T.S. and Creative Memories that sell supplies and can help you choose supplies and offer creative guidance. Check your yellow pages for these companies. Current is another great source of materials. They can be accessed on the Internet at www.current.com.

Here are a few basic tips for building your memory book.

1. Choose a good album to hold your memories. Creative Memories and D.O.T.S. both offer wonderful albums. Also make sure to use acid-free papers and supplies whenever possible. When papers are acid-free, they will not damage your photographs over time.
2. Collect all the materials that you think you would like to include. The possibilities are endless—postcards, words clipped from magazines, photos, special poems—anything that you like can be included.
3. Sort the items you have gathered until you see a natural progression take form. You may want to move through the book chronologically, or another theme may occur to you.
4. Gather stencils, stickers, stamps, and papers to use as decorations. Craft and scrapbooking stores are obvious suppliers. Additionally, office supply stores and stores like K-Mart, Wal-Mart, and Target often have good selection at reasonable prices.

5. Choose the materials you would like to use for a given page. Lay them out and move them around until you are comfortable with the design. If you have problems coming up with ideas for layout, consult one of the aforementioned magazines.

6. Take your time. There is no need to try and rush through the process of creating a memory book. Many people find joy in the "putzing" and creating. It may be a book that you continually add to throughout your lifetime.

Online Memorials

The Internet has created new ways to share, cherish, and remember our loved ones through online memorials. Videos, text entries, recordings, music, and photographs can be combined into a permanent web page to memorialize and remember the deceased.

This also helps for younger members of a family when they are growing up and may want to know about a deceased relative who died when the child was very young, etc. For more information visit www.legacy.com or www.muchloved.com

Visualization

Creative visualization can be a wonderful way to calm our mind and body. When our body is relaxed, we can play calming, healing, and encouraging "movies" on the screen of our mind. These movies or imaginings can promote healing, forgiveness, and peace.

Visualization may take a while to get used to. The first time you try it, you may feel you aren't "getting anywhere." Give yourself some time. Like any exercise, visualization takes practice. Also, you may want to do your visualizations while lying on the floor or sitting in a chair. If you do them in bed, you could very likely fall asleep, since the process is extremely relaxing.

To begin, follow the whole body relaxation from the calming exercise. When your body is relaxed and you do not feel any excess tension, begin your visualization.

As you do the exercises, thoughts and images may come to you that would be valuable to record. For this reason, it's a good idea to keep a visualization journal nearby.

Following are some visualization ideas. Choose one that feels comfortable to you or create one of your own. Feeding these positive messages into your mind will help reduce anxiety and depression—and help you to feel more joy and peace in life.

Visualize yourself using your grief in a creative way and in a positive setting. Notice what you are doing, who is around you, how you feel, and what you are seeing.

What did you see during this visualization?

_____

_____

_____

If you feel guilt for the death, imagine blowing all the guilt within you into a balloon. See the guilt move out of your body, up through your lungs, and into the balloon. See the balloon getting larger and larger until it contains all of your guilt. Hold on to the string of the balloon tightly, feeling all your guilt one last time. Then let it go. Watch the balloon carry the guilt away from you. You can use this same visualization with any other emotion that you want to get rid of—hatred, anger, jealousy, or revenge, to name a few.

How did you feel about the visualization?

_____

_____

_____

_____

Asking Questions through Visualization

If you want to communicate with the deceased or want to feel their presence, visualize them sitting in familiar surroundings. Go to them with your question or concern and let an exchange take place.

What question would you like to ask?

_____

_____

_____

After your visualization, record your "answer."

_____

_____

_____

_____

_____

_____

_____

_____

_____

_____

_____

_____

_____

_____

Important Things to Remember on the Pathway

- **Grief knows no schedule.** Remember, if someone says something like, "It's time now to get on with your life," you have the right to say, "In my time and God's time, not in your time."

- **If you want to wear black you can.** You can also wear any other color you want during the time you are grieving. **If you need isolation for a while that is okay.** You will be with people when you are ready.

- **Find a safe time and place to "go crazy" if you want to.** Go yell in the woods, throw rocks at trees, swear at the TV, or wear the deceased's clothes to bed.

- **Be kind to yourself.** Perfection is not necessary; there is no arriving, only going. There is no need to judge where you are in your journey. It is enough that you are traveling.

- **Make a commitment to your future.** Commitment enables you to bypass all your fears, mental escapes, and justifications, so that you can face whatever you are experiencing in the moment.

- **Get out of your own way.** The main block to healing from loss is the thought that we shouldn't be where we are, that we should already be further along in our growth than we perceive ourselves to be. Let these expectations go.

- **Affirm yourself.** Who you were and who you will be are insignificant compared to who you are.

- **Your life has not been a waste.** Every individual in your life reveals a part of you that you need to encounter and serves as a medium, through which you can see yourself, grow in awareness, and come closer to God within. Live every experience and every event you encounter as a learning opportunity, rather than as a threat of failure.

- **Fear is not always a bad thing.** If you allow yourself to experience fear fully, without trying to push it away, an inner shift takes place that initiates transformation.

There is no experience that exists in this life that does not have the power to lead you to greater knowledge and growth. Major loss can only become a vehicle for creating a renewed life when we stop thinking of it as a punishment and start to see it as a process. This process begins with the death of the relationship and proceeds through a period of grief and mourning, in which the death is recognized and accepted; the process ends with a rebirth from our experience.

Chapter Fifteen
Writing through Grief . . . Alone or within a Support Group

"What is needed is an impossible situation where one has to renounce one's own will and one's own wit and do nothing but wait and trust the impersonal power of growth and development. When you are up against a wall, be still and put down roots like a tree, until clarity comes from deeper sources to see over the wall."
—*Dr. Carl Jung*

Survivors can feel isolated and may experience a resultant loss of identity. Some may experience not only the clearly defined stages in counselors' handbooks but also a lingering sadness. You may be aching for the deceased. Many people consult a pastoral counselor or grief therapist, but there are other sources—poetry, music, volunteer work, support groups, group therapy, self-help books, and a variety of useful professional therapies which can frequently provide solace in unexpected ways. We have explored some of these in this chapter. One therapy or self-help avenue may work better for you than another. We all have unique needs, and what will work best for you depends on your background and your belief system.

You may also want to work through this workbook with others. Sharing our experiences with one another can be a great step toward healing. In this chapter you will find some common forms of support and some exercises you can try.

On the following pages you'll find some valuable self-help exercises that can be done at any stage of the grieving process. You may want to purchase a special journal or blank book to record your exercises. It's important that you find a safe place to keep your writing so that you can write your true feelings, unobstructed. If you have small children, you may even consider a small safe. These are available at stores like Wal-Mart and Office Max and vary in price—but are affordable.

Many people find it helpful to create a writing ritual. Some people like to write upon waking, others like to clear their head at the end of the day, and still others like to write both in the morning and evening. Experiment to find what works best for you. If writing daily is too much, write whenever the spirit moves you. I encourage to you to try writing daily, though—at least for a week or two. I think you'll find the benefits encouraging. Studies have shown that writing allows us to reach and unearth a part of us that we can't easily access through speaking with another person. After writing for several weeks, look back over your words—you will likely be surprised at what they reveal.

This section also contains answers to many of the frequently asked questions about self-help and therapy. This is a useful reference if you choose to seek professional help.

Journaling and Letter Writing

One of the most powerful tools for recovery is writing down your real thoughts and feelings in a journal—no editing or judgment. Writing a letter to the deceased can also be comforting. Some of your initial feelings will be quite strong or angry. Don't let this deter your efforts. You need to get those feelings out. After a while, your writing will turn softer as the emotional charge lessens. You have a unique and meaningful story to tell—the story of the beginning, middle, and ending of a relationship. Telling your story, writing it in a journal, creating poems, hearing others' stories . . . these are some ways we heal. No one has to read what you wrote for this exercise to work, although you may want to read portions of your journal to your support group members. One woman I spoke with said, "What worked best for me was to keep a daily gratitude journal so I could see that my life was full of more than just grief and loss. It helped me feel more balance and gave me a perspective that was empowering."

In her book, *The Fruitful Darkness*, Joan Halifax reflects on our collective as well as personal stories when she writes, "Stories are our protectors, like our immune system, defending against attacks of debilitating alienation . . . They are the connective tissue between culture and nature, self and other, life and death, that sew the worlds together, and in telling, the soul quickens and comes alive."

In his classic book, *Reaching Out*, Henri Nouwen writes that though our own story "can be hard to tell, full of disappointments and frustrations, deviations and stagnations . . . it is the only story we have and there will be no hope for the future when the past remains unconfessed, unreceived, and misunderstood."

Don't put any expectations or limitations on your writing—simply write. If you find it hard to get started, set a timer for five minutes and write anything that comes to mind. Don't stop. The writing may not make sense or be coherent, but it will help you get used to placing words on paper. Don't worry about spelling, grammar, or style—just get the words out. Try doing a five-minute writing exercise each morning when you wake or at night before going to bed. Try your first five-minute freewrite in the space provided on the following page. Use additional sheets of paper if necessary.

Freewrite

Devotions and Journaling

For those of you who would appreciate guidance from the Bible in your journaling, there is a wonderful Internet site at GriefShare. The area is called "On Your Own: Daily Help and Encouragement." The area guides you to sections of the Bible that are relevant to the feelings, emotions, and questions a person deals with during grief. The site offers thirteen weeks of personal devotions. Each week contains five daily Bible studies and suggestions for further reading. Each day also has an "In Your Life" area, which asks you questions to help you identify where you are in your journey from mourning to joy. You can access this tool at www.griefshare.com.

Take the time to find a way to tell your story. Listen to your story. Listen to the stories of others.

Poetry

Poetry creates a bridge of feelings between the material world and the world of creativity and spirit. Visiting and/or joining a poetry group can have an extraordinary effect on the way we heal our grief. Poets, by definition, get to the raw feelings behind the masks we all wear. When we are wearing the mask of grief, we may feel that others cannot possibly know the pain we are experiencing, yet we must still continue living day to day in spite of our tremendous loss. As a result, we may feel out of touch with friends who have not experienced such a loss. We may feel that the strength of our feelings is unacceptable to others. Yet feelings are the dynamic force behind poetry groups. Within these groups you will find a welcome and sensitive home for the expression of your grief through the written and spoken word.

Search the Internet for "Artists Salons" and/or "Poetry" in your state; also check your local paper for poetry readings. Attend the readings and ask participants about other local events in your area.

You can also write poetry on your own. Many books exist that can fuel creativity and offer guidance. Check the writing/reference section at your local bookstore. It can be extremely cleansing to spend a morning, once a week, at a café or park writing poetry in a beautiful journal. Don't worry about form—just creatively put down words to express yourself. Write poetry.

In the book, The *Poet's Companion: A Guide to the Pleasures of Writing Poetry,* author's Kim Addonizio and Dorianne Laux have a specific section on death and grief. They offer ten suggestions for working with this subject. "Write a poem about a ritual that accompanies a death. It might be about a traditional funeral, a wake, or some more private or individual observance. If you find an occasion for joy of beauty in the midst of mourning, include it." Another suggestion is, "If you own some object that used to belong to someone who is no longer alive, describe it in detail, along with your memories or images about how that person used it. You might also talk about how it is used in the present."

The Gratitude Journal

In her best-selling book, *Simple Abundance: A Daybook of Comfort and Joy*, Sarah Ban Breathnach advocates the use of a gratitude journal. She cites this as "a tool that could change the quality of your life beyond belief." We completely agree. This is how Sarah explains the gratitude journal:

> "I have a beautiful blank book and each night before I go to bed, I write down five things that I can be grateful about that day. Some days my list will be filled with amazing things, most days just simple joys. 'Mikey got lost in a fierce storm but I found him shivering, wet but unharmed. I listened to Puccini while cleaning and remembered how much I love opera.'
>
> Other days—rough ones—I might think that I don't have five things to be grateful for, so I'll write down my basics: my health, my husband and daughter, their health, my animals, my home, my friends, and the comfortable bed that I'm about to get into, as well as the fact that the day's over. That's okay. Real life isn't always going to be perfect or go our way, but the recurring acknowledgment of what is working in our lives can help us not only survive but surmount our difficulties."

Recognizing the positives in our lives is especially important when we are engulfed in dark times. We often focus so heavily on our loss and what isn't going right, that we can't see any of the good things. For the first few months, it will be extremely difficult to find the positives, but after that initial time period, we need to begin looking again—no matter how simple these positives might be. Your list might include something as basic as "I was able to get out of bed today." What's important is that we be open to the fact that there are positives. By recognizing them, we attract more positives to our life.

For one week, keep your own gratitude journal recording five positive things that happen each day. At the end of the week, write what you learned from this exercise. It will likely be an activity you will want to continue!

Day One

_____

_____

_____

_____

Day Two

_____

_____

_____

_____

Day Three

_____

_____

_____

_____

Day Four

_____

_____

_____

_____

Day Five

_____

_____

_____

_____

Day Six

_____

_____

_____

_____

Day Seven

_____

_____

_____

_____

What I learned from the gratitude journal exercise:

_____

_____

_____

_____

_____

_____

_____

_____

_____

I know I need group support but what kind of group is best for me? How do I know which one is right?

A support or therapy group can be the ideal place for you to explore your feelings. Your previous circle of mutual friends may no longer be available to you and a support group will be valuable in helping you re-establish your place in the world. Let's explore the basic group types.

A professionally led support group is organized and facilitated by a psychotherapist, pastoral counselor, psychologist, social worker, or other mental health professional. You should feel supported and nurtured without judgment in this type of group. A fee may be charged since it is run by professionals.

A peer-led support group is just that—led by someone who has experienced sudden death of a loved one and has decided to help others. Usually it is someone who is at least a year or two into the grieving process. There is normally no fee, or perhaps a donation will be requested of you.

A professionally led therapy group requires you to be in private counseling with the professional running the group and is an adjunct to your therapy work. You may also feel supported and nurtured in this group, but the therapist may challenge you on some of the beliefs you have that get in the way of your healing.

Many organizations form groups. Hospitals and religious organizations sometimes sponsor these groups. Therapists and social workers also form groups. Finding the right group for you will be easier if you pay attention to your intuition during and after the first meeting. At a time when we aren't sure of our ability to make decisions, trust your gut feelings to guide you. And don't give up—keep trying until you find the right fit.

Questions for a Support Group

These are some questions you will want to ask the person who is in charge:

Is there a fee? _____

How often do you meet? _____

Is there an attendance requirement? _____

Is it mandatory to share or speak at the group? _____

_____

How many people are there in the group? (If the group is larger than ten, you may not get your needs met as readily. There is only so much time for each person.) _____

Is the group for men/women only? A group consisting of women only will help women develop supportive female relationships; and a group of all men will help men safely express their feelings.

_____

Allow the group the opportunity to "give" to you. Work on believing you have earned the right to receive. Don't be afraid to talk about or express your feelings. After all, that's why you came. You will not receive the support you came for if you hold back. Think about friends in your life and realize that it was with time that the level and depth of their friendship was revealed—the same is true in a group experience.

Use the following space to record information you learn about the support groups you talk to.

_____

_____

_____

_____

_____

_____

_____

_____

Try the following exercise. The first time you go to a support or therapy group, take a pencil and paper with you. Either during or immediately after, jot down words that describe how you are feeling. Pay close attention to your feelings. Now do this again the second time you go, and once more the third time. Are you still feeling the same as you did the first time and second time? If your experience is mostly positive, continue with the group. If you notice you have written mostly about anxiety, fear, stress, or shame, then stop going. Keep looking until you find a group that gives you positive feelings. Remember, a group is meant to be part of your extended support system. Take into account however, that you will not always feel uplifted each time you go, because the grieving process takes time, and it is full of its own ups and downs.

The stories of loss we have heard are as diverse as fingerprints—each one slightly different from the next. When we gather with those who attend and begin sharing, the connections, one to another, are astounding. Regardless of where we are in the process of grieving, or how we lost our loved one, we become supportive, relating to and recognizing each other's pain almost immediately. This sense of community and acceptance is vitally important to our spiritual and emotional healing.

On the following page, you'll find some questions that are useful for evaluating a support group.

Chapter Sixteen
Resources and Support

"I give you what no thief can steal,
the memories of our times together:
the tender, love-filled moments"
—*Edward Hays, Prayers for a Planetary Pilgrim*

In the first edition we provided over fifty pages of supportive resources. We have now created an online library of grief support links and articles in order to keep our ever-expanding information base current while providing easy access by topic.

In this section we provide information on some general resources and support available to the bereaved. For a printable or searchable complete list of resources, including links to Internet support, please visit us at www.griefsteps.com.

Support for Loss of a Partner

American Association of Retired Persons (AARP)
601 E St., NW, Washington, D.C. 20049. 1–800–424–3410 (1–888-OUR-AARP). AARP Grief and Loss Programs offer a wide variety of resources and information on bereavement issues for adults of all ages and their families. Services include: one-to-one peer outreach, a grief course, bereavement support groups, informational booklets and brochures, and online support. www.aarp.org/griefandloss.

WidowNet (Internet Resource)
This is the most comprehensive site we've found for those who are widowed. WidowNet is an information and self-help resource created for, and by, widows and widowers. "Topics covered include grief, bereavement, recovery, and other information helpful to people, of all ages, religious backgrounds, and sexual orientations, who have suffered the death of a spouse or life partner." You can access the site at www.widownet.org. They also have a chat room and message board.

Books

How to Go On Living When Someone You Love Dies by Therese A. Rando, PhD, 1988, New York, Lexington Books—Includes suggestions for ways to deal with sudden or anticipated death. Offers self-help techniques to work on unfinished business, take care of the self, and when to get help from others. Leads you through the painful but necessary process of grieving and helps you find the best way for yourself. Offers guidance to help you move into your new life without forgetting your treasured past.

Living with Loss: Meditations for Grieving Widows by Ellen Sue Stern, 1995, Dell Publishing, NY—This book, small enough to fit in a purse, is full of supportive and empowering reflections. This daily companion is designed to help you cope today, cherish yesterday, and thrive tomorrow.

Support for Grieving Children

Camp "Good Grief"

Camp "Good Grief" is a summer camp program which offers grief education workshops and provides support and understanding for youth ages six through thirteen who have experienced the death of a sibling, parent, grandparent, or close friend. The camp is held in Lake Worth, FL. For more information, visit the website at www.campgoodgrief.org or call (561) 416–5059.

KIDSAID (Internet Resource)

KIDSAID is an extension of GriefNet, a comprehensive Internet community that has provided support to over three million people in the last year. The KIDSAID area provides a safe environment for kids and their parents to find information and ask questions. To learn more about KIDSAID, visit GriefNet at www.griefnet.org or kidsaid.com/about.html.

Books for Children and Teens and Their Caregivers

Bereaved Children and Teens: A Support Guide for Parents and Professionals by Earl A. Grollman, Beacon Press, 1996—Explores the ways that parents and professionals can help young people cope with grief. Topics covered include what children can understand about death at different ages, the special problems of grieving teenagers, how to explain Protestant, Catholic, or Jewish beliefs about death in ways that children can understand, and more.

Don't Despair on Thursdays! by Adolph Moser, Ed.D., Western Psychological Services. Geared toward children ages four through twelve, this gentle book lets children know that it's normal to grieve in response to loss and that grief may last more than a few days or weeks. Offers practical suggestions that children can use, day by day, to cope with the emotional pain they feel. Young readers will be comforted by the reassuring text and colorful illustrations.

Part of Me Died, Too: Stories of Creative Survival among Bereaved Children and Teenagers by Virginia Lynn Fry, 1995, Dutton Children's Books, NY—Eleven true stories about young people who experienced the loss of family members or friends in a variety of ways including murder, suicide, and accident. Includes writings, drawings, farewell projects, rituals, and other creative activities to help younger children and teens bring their feelings out into the open.

The Grieving Child: A Parents Guide by Helen Fitzgerald. Fireside, 1992—Compassionate advice for helping a child cope with the death of a loved one. Also addresses visiting the seriously ill, using age-appropriate language, funerals, and more.

Support for the Loss of a Child

Bereaved Parents of the USA

This national organization was founded in 1995 to aid and support bereaved parents and their families who are struggling to survive their grief after the death of a child. Information and referrals, a newsletter, phone support, conferences, and meetings are available. They also offer assistance in starting a support group. You may contact them at P.O. Box 95, Park Forest, IL 60466 or by calling (708) 748–7866 or http://www.bereavedparentsusa.org/.

Mothers in Sympathy and Support (MISS)

From their website: "The mission of Mothers in Sympathy & Support is to allow a safe haven for parents to share their grief after the death of a child. It is our hope that within these pages you discover courage, faith, friendship, and love. Grief education for parents and professionals is our main focus. Our child has changed our lives forever. Come with us and get lost in our pages . . . find healing, honesty, hope, and a rediscovery of yourself." Visit www.misschildren.org/.

SHARE: Pregnancy & Infant Loss Support, Inc.

This group offers support to those who have lost a child during pregnancy or infancy. Their extensive website offers a chat room and many valuable reading areas. Additionally, they offer a free newsletter. You can visit their website at www.nationalshareoffice.com/ or you may contact them at: National SHARE Office, St. Joseph Health Center, 300 First Capitol Drive, St. Charles, MO 63301–2893, Phone: (800) 821–6819 or (636) 947–6164. All of SHARE's information packets, correspondence, and support is free of charge for bereaved parents. They also publish a bi-monthly newsletter that is available to bereaved parents.

Books

A Broken Heart Still Beats: When Your Child Dies edited by Anne McCracken and Mary Semel, Hazelden, 1998—Edited by two mothers who have lost a child, this book combines articles and excerpts—some fiction, some nonfiction—that featured the death of a child. A brief introduction to each chapter describes a different stage of the grieving process and how it affected their lives.

The Worst Loss: How Families Heal from the Death of a Child by Barbara D. Rosof, Henry Holt & Co., Inc., 1994—The death of a child overwhelms many people. This book describes the losses that the death of a child brings to parents and siblings, as well as potential PTSD reactions and work of grief. A very thorough and wise book. One of our favorite books on the topic.

Support for Loss through Suicide

American Suicide Foundation

This national organization offers state-by-state directories of survivor support groups for families and friends of suicide. Contact them by e-mail at inquiry@afsp.org or write to **120 Wall Street, 22nd Floor,** New York, NY 10005; or call 1 (888) 333-AFSP.

Friends for Survival, Inc.

Organized by and for survivors, this non-profit group offers its services at no cost to those who have lost a loved one to suicide. Resources include a newsletter, referrals to local support groups, a list of suggested resources, and more. You may contact them at Friends for Survival, Inc., P.O. Box 214463, Sacramento, California 95821. Or call (916) 392–0664. http://www.friendsforsurvival.org/.

Books

Healing After the Suicide of a Loved One by Ann Smolin, John Guinan, Fireside, 1993—The authors address the special needs and emotions of the survivors and those affected by the suicide of a loved one. It explores the natural grief, and the added guilt, rage, and shame that dealing with a suicide often engenders. Includes a directory of worldwide support groups.

No Time to Say Goodbye: Surviving the Suicide of a Loved One by Carla Fine, Doubleday, 1997—Suicide is something most people are unable to talk about, which makes the pain all the more unbearable. Written by a suicide survivor, this book explores the overwhelming feelings of guilt, shame, anger, and loneliness that are shared by survivors. Offers guidance to those who were left behind and are struggling to pick up the pieces of their shattered lives.

Why Suicide? Answers to 200 of the Most Frequently Asked Questions about Suicide, Attempted Suicide and Assisted Suicide by Eric Marcus, Harper San Francisco, 1996—No matter what the circumstances surrounding suicide, those of us who are affected are left with difficult and disturbing questions. This book provides thoughtful, comprehensive answers to two hundred of the most frequently asked questions about suicide, attempted suicide, and assisted suicide.

Internet Support for Siblings

Adult Sibling Grief (Internet Resource)

This website reaches out to grieving adults who have lost a sibling. They offer resources, a special remembrance area, message boards, and support groups. Access the site at www.adultsiblinggrief.com.

SOLOS-Sibs Suicide (Internet Resource)

An email support group for adults who have lost a brother or sister to suicide at any age. Discussion revolves around mutual grief support and sibling survivor issues. health.groups.yahoo.com/group/SOLOS-sibs/

Mourning Our Brothers and Sisters (Internet Resource)

Offers message board support and the opportunity to connect with others who may understand what it's like to be a surviving sibling. health.groups.yahoo.com/group/M_O_B_S_/.

General Bereavement Support

Beyond Indigo (Internet Resource)

This site offers comprehensive support to individuals who are grieving and those who want to help them. They have a monthly newsletter that is delivered via email and online memorials. They also have message boards, polls, grief tools, advice columns, and articles. Check out their offerings at www.beyondindigo.com.

Concerns of Police Survivors, Inc. (COPS)

This national association provides services to surviving friends and families of law enforcement officers killed in the line of duty. COPS can be contacted at P.O. Box 3199, Camdenton, MO 65020; or by calling (573) 346–4911 or by email at cops@nationalcops.org.

GriefNet (Internet Resource)

GriefNet is an Internet community consisting of almost fifty email support groups and two websites. Over three million people have visited the website in the last year. A very supportive site. Visit it at www.griefnet.org.

Grief Share (Internet Resource)

This Internet resource provides a comprehensive support group directory, special resources, and a bookstore. Additionally, they have a wonderful area about journaling and a six-week-guide with a Christian focus that includes scriptures, ideas for writing, and journal pages you can print. Visit their site at www.griefshare.org.

Tom Golden's Grief and Healing Discussions Page (Internet Resource)

This site uses a web message board where you can post and respond to issues of grief and loss. Access the message board at www.webhealing.com/forums/.

Transformations (Internet Resource)

This well-designed site offers support in many areas, including grief. They offer a chat area and a schedule of events, as well as a place to share your thoughts, stories, poetry, and more. You can access the site at www.transformations.com/contents.html.

Other Recommended Books by Topic

General Books for Adults

A Time to Grieve: Meditations for Healing after the Death of a Loved One by Carol Staudacher, Harper San Francisco, 1994—Three hundred and sixty-five daily readings offer comfort, insight, and hope. This book is written specifically for people after the death of a loved one, however it is appropriate for anyone who still copes with the effects of a loss of any kind. A great gift for yourself or a grieving friend.

Beyond Grief by Carol Staudacher, New Harbinger Publications, 1987—This book is about understanding and then coping with loss, with clearly stated suggestions for each part of the grieving process. Written both for the bereaved and the helping professional, it combines supportive personal stories with a step-by-step approach to recovery. *Beyond Grief* acknowledges the path, reassures, and counsels. Includes guidelines to create support groups and guidelines for helping others. It says to the grieving person: you are not alone, you can get through the pain, and there is a path back to feeling alive again.

Companion through Darkness: Inner Dialogues on Grief by Stephanie Ericsson, HarperPerennial Library, 1993—As a result of her own experience with many kinds of loss, the author offers an intimate, touching guide for those in grief. The book combines excerpts from her own diary writings with brief essays.

The Courage to Grieve by Judy Tatelbaum—This book covers many aspects of grief and resolution. Divided into five sections, it explores the grief experience and creative recovery.

What to Do When a Loved One Dies: A Practical and Compassionate Guide to Dealing with Death on Life's Terms, by Eva Shaw, Dickens Press, 1994—Presents excellent guidelines describing what to do when a death occurs. It has an extensive listing of support groups, resources, and other sources of help. The approach is extremely detailed and includes sections on dealing with catastrophic deaths.

Books about the Loss of a Friend

Grieving the Death of a Friend by Harold Ivan Smith, Augsburg Fortress Publications, 1996—The death of a friend is one of the most significant but unrecognized experiences of grief in American culture. This unique new book moves with, rather than against, the natural grief process by exploring its many aspects—the friending, the passing, the burying, the mourning, the remembering, and the reconciling.

When a Friend Dies: A Book for Teens about Grieving and Healing by Marilyn E. Gootman, Ed.D., 1994, Free Spirit Publishing, Minneapolis, MN—A small, powerful book whose author has seen her own children suffer from the death of a friend. She knows firsthand what teenagers go through when another teen dies. Very easy to read, some of the questions dealt with include: How long will this last? Is it wrong to go to parties and have fun? How can I find a counselor or therapist? What is normal?

Books about Losing a Parent

How to Survive the Loss of a Parent: A Guide for Adults by Lois F. Akner, Catherine Whitney, 1994, William Morrow & Co.—Therapist and author, Lois Akner, explains why the loss of a parent is different from other losses and using examples from her experience, shows how it is possible to work through the grief.

Losing a Parent: Passage to a New Way of Living by Alexandra Kennedy, Harper San Francisco, 1991—Based on the author's personal experience, she writes on topics such as keeping a journal, saying goodbye, tending to your wounds, and the "living parent within you."

Mid-Life Orphan: Facing Life's Changes Now That Your Parents Are Gone by Jane Brooks. Berkely Books, 1999—Many mid-life orphans feel isolated, even abandoned, when their parents dies, but they also learn how to cope and extract life lessons from their experience. This book focuses on a loss that has been a fact of life for centuries, but has moved to the forefront as baby boomers, who represent one-third of the U.S. population, are forced to deal with this age of loss.

May you see the light where there was only darkness, hope where there seemed nothing but despair, may your fear be replaced with faith and insight, may you feel some victory in the defeat and a sense of the sacred web into which we are all woven. Most of all may you stay in tune with your capacity to love in life even as you are engulfed by death.

Bibliography

Adrienne, Carol. *The Purpose of Your Life Experiential Guide.* William Morrow, 1999.

Akner, Lois F. Whitney, Catherine (contributor). *How to Survive The Loss of a Parent: A Guide for Adults.* Quill, 1994.

Albertson, Sandy. *Endings and Beginnings.* Random House, 1980.

American Association of Retired Persons Brochure, *Frequently asked Questions by the Widowed.*

American Association of Retired Persons Brochure, *On Being Alone.*

American Association of Retired Persons website article, "Common Reactions to Loss."

Arent Ruth. *Helping Children Grieve.* Sourcebooks, 2007.

Balch M.D., James F. and Phyllis A. Balch C.N.C. *Prescription for Nutritional Healing.* Avery Publishing Group, 1997.

Bowlby, John. *Loss: Sadness and Depression.* HarperCollins, 1980.

Bowlby J: Processes of mourning. *Int J Psychoanal 42:* 1961.

Bowlby J: Attachment and Loss. Vols. 1–3, New York: Basic Books, Inc., 1969–1980.

Bozarth, Alla Renee. *A Journey through Grief: Specific Help to Get You through the Most Difficult Stages of Grief.* Hazelden, 1994.

Bramblett, John. *When Goodbye Is Forever: Learning to Live Again after the Loss of a Child.* Ballantine, 1997.

Breathnach, Sarah Ban. *Simple Abundance: A Daybook of Comfort and Joy.* New York: Warner, 1995.

Challem, Jack. "Relief for Chronic Fatigue: How NADH Can Help." *Let's Live,* October 1999. pp. 48–50.

Chevallier, Andrew. *The Encyclopedia of Medicinal Plants.* Dorling Kindersley, 1996.

Childs-Gowell, Elaine. *Good Grief Rituals: Tools for Healing.* Station Hill, 1992.

Coffin, Margaret M. *Death in Early America.* Thomas Nelson, 1976.

Collins, Judy. *Singing Lessons: A Memoir of Love, Loss, Hope, and Healing.* Pocket Books, 1998.

Conway, Jim. *Men in Midlife Crisis.* Chariot Victor, 1997.

Cunningham, Linda. *Grief and the Adolescent.* TAG: Teen Age Grief.

Curry, Cathleen L. *When Your Spouse Dies: A Concise and Practical Source of Help and Advice.* Ave Maria Press, 1990.

Deits, Bob. *Life After Loss: A Personal Guide Dealing with Death, Divorce, Job Change, and Relocation.* Fisher, 1992.

Doka, Kenneth J (editor). Kenneth, Kola J. (editor). Hospice Foundation of America. *Living with Grief after Sudden Loss: Suicide, Homicide, Accident, Heart Attack, Stroke.* Taylor and Francis, 1996.

Edelman, Hope. *Motherless Daughters: The Legacy of Loss.* Delta, 1995.

Editors of Prevention Health Books. *Prevention's Healing with Vitamins.* Rodale Press, 1996.

Ericsson, Stephanie. *Companion through the Darkness: Inner Dialogues on Grief.* Harperperennial Library, 1993.

Felber, Marta. *Grief Expressed: When a Mate Dies.* Lifeword, 1997.

Fine, Carla. *No Time to Say Goodbye: Surviving the Suicide of a Loved One.* Main Street Books, 1999.

"Final Details." Brochure by The American Association of Retired Persons.

Fitzgerald, Helen. *The Mourning Handbook: The Most Comprehensive Resource Offering Practical and Compassionate Advice on Coping with All Aspects of Death and Dying.* Fireside, 1995.

"Forgotten Mourners: after the death of a brother or sister, family members often don't realize the extent of the siblings' grief." *The Journal News,* July 29, 1999.

Freud, Sigmund. From a letter to Ludwig Binswanger who had lost a son.

Friedman, Russell and John W. James. *The Grief Recovery Handbook: The Action Program for Moving Beyond Death, Divorce, and Other Losses.* HarperCollins, 1998.

Fumia, Molly. *Safe Passage : Words to Help the Grieving Hold Fast and Let Go.* Conaris Press, 1992.

Ginsburg, Genevieve Davis. *Widow to Widow: Thoughtful Practical Ideas for Rebuilding Your Life.* Fisher Books, 1995.

Grey, John. *Men Are from Mars, Women Are from Venus: A Practical Guide for Improving Communication and Getting What You Want in Your Relationships.* Harpercollins, 1992.

Golden, Tom LCSW. "A Family Ritual for the Year Anniversary." Tom Golden Grief Column.

Goldman, Linda. *Breaking the Silence: A Guide to Help Children with Complicated Grief.* Western Psychological Services.

Gootman, Marilyn. *When a Friend Dies: A Book for Teens about Grieving and Healing.* Free Spirit Publishing, 1994.

Goulston, Mark MD and Philip Goldberg. *Get Out of Your Own Way.* Perigee, 1996.

Grollman, Earl A. *Living When A Loved One Has Died.* Beacon Press, 1995.

Halifax, Joan. *The Fruitful Darkness: Reconnecting with the Body of the Earth.* Harper San Francisco, 1994.

Harris, Maxine. *The Loss That is Forever: The Lifelong Impact of the Early Death of a Mother or Father.* Plume, 1996.

Hays, Edward M. *Prayers for a Planetary Pilgrim: A Personal Manual for Prayer and Ritual.* Forest of Peace Books, 1998.

Heegaard, Marge Eaton. *Coping with Death and Grief.* Lerner Publications, 1990.

Hendricks, Lois Lindsey. *Dreams that Help You Mourn.* Resource Publications, 1997.

Henricks, Gay. *The Learning to Love Yourself Workbook.* Prentice Hall, 1992.

Hewett, John H. *After Suicide.* Westminster John Knox, 1980.

Johnson, Elizabeth A. *As Someone Dies: A Handbook for the Living.* Hay House, 1995.

Kennedy, Alexandra. *Losing a Parent: Passage to a New Way of Living.* Harper San Francisco, 1991.

King, Marlene. "The Surrogate Dreamers." *Intuition.* January/February 1998.

Kolf, June Cezra. *How Can I Help?: How to Support Someone Who Is Grieving.* Fisher Books, 1999.

Kubler-Ross, M.D., Elisabeth. *On Children and Death: How Children and Their Parents Can and Do Cope with Death.* Simon and Schuster, 1997.

Kushner, Harold S. *When Bad Things Happen to Good People.*

L'Engle, Madeleine. *Sold into Egypt: Joseph's Journey into Human Being.* Harold Shaw, 1989.

Lerner, Harriet. *The Dance of Anger: A Woman's Guide to Changing the Patterns of Intimate Relationships.* HarperCollins, 1997.

Livingston M.D., Gordon. *Only Spring: On Mourning the Death of My Son.* Marlowe & Company, 1999.

Mabe, Juliet. *Words to Comfort, Words to Heal: Poems and Mediations for Those Who Grieve.*

Marshall, Fiona. *Losing A Parent: A Personal Guide to Coping with That Special Grief That Comes with Losing a Parent.* Fisher Books, 1993.

Marx, Robert J. and Susan Davidson. *Facing the Ultimate Loss: Coping with the Death of a Child.* Sourcebooks, 2007.

Matsakis, Aphrodite. *I Can't Get Over It: A Handbook for Trauma Survivors.* New Harbinger Publications, 1996.

Matsakis, Aphrodite. *Trust After Trauma: A Guide to Relationships for Survivors and Those Who Love Them.* New Harbinger Publications, 1998.

Mechner, Vicki. *Healing Journeys: The Power of Rubenfield Synergy.* Omniquest, 1998.

Melrose, Andrea LaSonder (editor). *Nine Visions: A Book of Fantasies.* Seabury Press, 1983.

Mental Health Association in Waukesha County. "Grief After Suicide." Pewaukee, Wisconsin.

Miller PhD, Jack. *Healing Our Losses: A Journal for Working through Your Grief.* Resource Publications.

Mitchard, Jacquelyn. *The Deep End of the Ocean.* Penguin, 1999.

Noel, Brook. *Shadows of a Vagabond.* Champion Press, 1998.

Noel, Brook. *Grief Steps.* Champion Press, Ltd., 2003.

Noel, Brook with Art Klein. *The Single Parent Resource.* Champion Press, 1998.

Nouwen, Henri J. *Reaching Out: The Three Movements of the Spiritual Life.* Image Books, 1986.

O'Neil, Anne-Marie; Schneider, Karen S. and Alex Tresnowski. "Starting Over." *People* magazine, October 4, 1999. p 125.

Overbeck, Buz and Joanie Overbeck. "Where Life Surrounds Death." Adapted from Helping Children Cope with Loss.

Parkes CM: Bereavement: *Studies of Grief in Adult Life. 2nd ed.,* Madison: International Universities Press Inc., 1987.

Parkes CM: Bereavement as a psychosocial transition: processes of adaptation to change. *J Soc Issues 44,* 1988.

Prend, Ashley Davis. *Transcending Loss: Understanding the Lifelong Impact of Grief and How to Make It Meaningful.* Berkely, 1997.

Rando PhD, Therese A. *Treatment of Complicated Mourning.* Research Press, 1993.

Rando PhD, Therese A. *How to Go on Living When Someone You Love Dies.* Bantam, 1991.

Rilke, Rainer Maria. *Letters to a Young Poet.* WW Norton, 1994.

Rosof, Barbara D. *The Worst Loss: How Families Heal from the Death of a Child.* Henry Holt, 1995.

Sachs, Judith with Lendon H. Smith. *Nature's Prozac: Natural Therapies and Techniques to Rid Yourself of Anxiety, Depression, Panic Attacks & Stress.* Prentice Hall, 1998.

Sanders, Dr. Catherine M. *Surviving Grief.* John Wiley, 1992.

Schiff, Harriet Sarnoff. *The Bereaved Parent.* Viking, 1978.

Shaw, Eva. *What to Do When A Loved One Dies: A Practical and Compassionate Guide to Dealing with Death on Life's Terms.* Dickens Press, 1994.

Staudacher, Carol. A *Time to Grieve : Meditations for Healing After the Death of a Loved One.* Harper San Francisco, 1994.

Staudacher, Carol. *Beyond Grief: A Guide for Recovering from the Death of a Loved One.* New Harbinger Publications, 1987.

Staudacher, Carol. *Men and Grief: A Guide for Men Surviving the Death of a Loved One: A Resource for Caregivers and Mental Health Professionals.* New Harbinger Publications, 1991.

Stearn, Ellen Sue. *Living With Loss: Meditations for Grieving Widows (Days of Healing, Days of Change).* Bantam, 1995.

Stoltz PhD, Paul G. *Adversity Quotient: Turning Obstacles into Opportunities.* John Wiley & Sons, 1999.

Tatelbaum, Judy. *The Courage to Grieve.* HarperCollins, 1984.

Temes, Dr. Roberta. *Living with an Empty Chair: A Guide through Grief.* New Horizon, 1992.

Viorst, Judith. *Necessary Losses: The Loves, Illusions, Dependencies, and Impossible Expectations That All of Us Have to Give Up in Order to Grow.* Fireside, 1998.

Webb, Denise, PhD "Supplement News." *Prevention,* October 1999. p 61.

Westberg, Granger E. *Good Grief.* Fortress Press, 1971.

Worwood, Valerie Ann. *The Fragrant Mind.* New World Library, 1996.

Zarda, Dan and Marcia Woodaard. *Forever Remembered.* Compendium, 1997.

Zunin M.D., Leornard M. and Hilary Stanton Zunin. *The Art of Condolence.* Harper Perennial Library, 1992.

www.griefsteps.com

Brook Noel's Grief Support Site

Grief Steps is my personal outreach to continue offering grief support services and free grief resources for those navigating through life after the death of a loved one. While each person's grief is unique, it is my belief that we need never be alone in the grief journey. Through Grief Steps, support is only a click or two away and available twenty-four hours a day, seven days a week.

Some of the resources you will find at Grief Steps include:

Online support groups
Online grief programs to work through the Grief Steps
Guides to create and lead a support group
Journaling pages
Internet links and printed lists of resources
Printable handouts
Topic-specific ebooks
Downloadable workbooks
Grief Steps Support Newsletter
Grief Online Support chats hosted by Brook Noel
Audios by Brook Noel on the grieving process
Helpful articles by Brook Noel and other experts on specific areas of grief
Visit www.griefsteps.com to learn more.

About the Authors

Pamela D. Blair, PhD

Dr. Blair earned her PhD in philosophy and a masters in metaphysics from the American Institute of Holistic Theology. She has certificates in Integrative Therapy and Therapeutic Touch, has studied at the New England Educational Institute and the Transformational Training Institute, and has a divinity degree from the New Seminary in New York, NY. As a therapist, she is known for her innovative personal growth workshops and support groups.

In addition to I Wasn't Ready to Say Goodbye, she has authored The Next Fifty Years: A Guide for Women at Midlife and Beyond (Hampton Roads Publishing Co.). A frequently invited guest on television, cable, and radio talk shows, Dr. Blair has appeared on CBS TV and is a contributing editor to me* Magazine, GriefNet.com, and Divorce Magazine. Visit her website at www.pamelablair.com

Brook Noel

Brook Noel is the author of nineteen books, specializing in life management, balance, and life transitions. Known for going "beyond the book," Noel uses many means to interact with and support her readers. She delivers free motivational podcasts, online Q&A chats, message board interaction, in-person free "coffees" when she travels, and four free newsletters with over one hundred thousand total subscribers. Noel's interactive grief outreach program, GriefSteps™ can be accessed at www.griefsteps.com "While some of my work deals with life's hardest blows, other work deals with the day-to-day stressors and challenges. My life experiences have taught me that today is what matters... right here and right now. I am committed to helping others reap the gift of today."

Noel has appeared on hundreds of media outlets, including CNN Headline News, ABC World News, FOX Friends, Woman's World, Parent's Journal, Town & Country, New York Post, "Ask Heloise," and Bloomberg Radio . Her work has been recognized by the Midwest Independent Publisher Awards, the Best Book Awards, and the IPPY Awards.Noel was recognized in 2003 as one of the 40 Top Most Influential Business People Under the Age of 40 by the Business Journal. She is a spokesperson for the Home Business Association and was chosen as one of ten entrepreneurs of the year.

Brook lives in Wisconsin with her husband, twelve-year-old daughter, one golden retriever, a black lab named "Kitty," and one very large cat named Tom. Visit her website at www.brooknoel.com